About the Cover

The pink triangle used as a motif in the cover design has been adopted by present-day lesbians and gays as a badge of resistance to bigotry and discrimination. The symbol dates back to Nazi Germany, which conducted campaigns of repression and persecution against homosexuals, gypsies and religious and political dissenters, in addition to their systematic plan of extermination against Jews. In Nazi concentration camps, homosexuals were required to wear a pink triangle, just as Jews were forced to wear a yellow star. Today the pink triangle recalls the larger context of the Nazi Holocaust and reminds us of the extremes to which hatred and discrimination can be carried when we do not stand up against them.

Bridges of Respect

Creating Support for Lesbian and Gay Youth

Written for the
American Friends Service Committee

Katherine Whitlock, Author
Rachael Kamel, Editor

Second edition, Copyright © July 1989 by
the American Friends Service Committee

ISBN: 0-910082-39-1

Designed by Barbara Benton
Printed in the United States of America

American Friends Service Committee
1501 Cherry Street
Philadelphia, PA 19102

Foreword

The American Friends Service Committee, which has published this guide, was founded in 1917 to put into practice the testimonies of the Religious Society of Friends (Quakers). These testimonies, which have evolved over three centuries, spring from a commitment to peace and justice for all human beings. The central concept of George Fox and Margaret Fell, founders of Quakerism—that there is a direct relationship between God and the individual, and that each person is therefore uniquely precious—leads naturally to a respect for human beings in all their great diversity and a concern that they be granted full freedom of life and expression.

Friends believe that, just as God spoke to the writers of the Scriptures, God continues to speak to us today: that there is a continuing revelation. Typically, a Quaker concern is born when an individual, often in the silence of the meeting for worship, becomes sensitive to the injustice and suffering of a group of people and expresses this concern to the meeting. If she or he is able to persuade the meeting to unite with the position stated, the meeting becomes an advocate and brings the concern to the attention of other Quaker bodies. Thus over a period of years, perhaps decades, a new Quaker testimony evolves.

Quaker concerns regarding injustices and violence experienced by lesbians and gay men began to emerge when members of local meetings had the courage to publicly disclose their sexual orientation and to tell of the discrimination and harassment they suffered as a result. In Great Britain, this experience led eleven Friends to write an essay called *Toward a Quaker View of Sex*, published in 1963 by the Home Service Committee of the Religious Society of Friends. In the early 1970s, a number of yearly and monthly meetings in the United States published minutes affirming the lesbian/gay struggle for civil rights. In those same years, gay men and lesbians within the American Friends Service Committee began to identify themselves publicly, to challenge injustices and stereotypes and to speak of their vision for change. As a result of the dialog that emerged, gay men and lesbians were included in the AFSC affirmative action plan for hiring, employment practices, committee membership and program development. In addition, a Lesbian and Gay Rights Task Force was established.

Many of the Friends who have taken a position in support of full recognition of and respect for lesbians and gays cite as a turning point in the development of new attitudes the experience of coming to know an individual gay man or lesbian. Deeply held stereotypes, some of them unconscious, melt away in the face of shared confidence and genuine friendship.

In my own case, learning about the real lives, struggles, dreams and strengths of lesbians and gay men—by reading their writings and listening to respected and beloved members of my own meeting as well as other Quaker groups—caused me to begin to reexamine my attitudes toward the varieties of expression of human sexuality and to commence the long journey toward complete acceptance of this aspect of human diversity. In the course of that journey, it becomes increasingly clear to me that the struggle is not simply to undo a form of oppression for others, but also to free myself from the fears and distortions that perpetuate injustice and keep people estranged from one another. I am hopeful that more and more Friends can share this first-hand experience of awakening and that the dialog among Friends will come to be based on real situations and real people.

Not all Friends have taken the same position. This is a concern of some, not a testimony of the whole Society. The Quaker testimonies we honor today were all born slowly, over a period of time. Not all Quakers were pacifists at the birth of the movement. George Fox told William Penn to wear his sword "as long as thou canst," leaving the moment of decision to Penn. Although a group of Friends in Germantown (now a part of Philadelphia) declared against slavery in 1688, it was not until 1776 that the Society as a whole decided that no Quaker could own a slave and Friends became active in the abolition movement. Opposition to the death penalty did not become a Quaker testimony until the nineteenth century. And, while Quaker women participated equally in the meeting house and as ministers, the Society did not unite behind the campaign for women's rights until the final suffrage campaigns in the early part of this century.

In the case of lesbian and gay rights, some Friends feel bound by what they understand to be the biblical injunctions against homosexuality. Other Friends have studied the often-cited biblical passages in the original and feel that they cannot be translated to apply literally to the present situation. Nor, in this view, do they override the greatest commandment: that we should love our God and our neighbors as ourselves. As the dialog continues, Friends endeavor to practice what they preach and to listen to one another with real respect.

Bridges of Respect contributes to the creation of that climate of respect, while providing youth workers with the tools they need to understand the young gays and lesbians who are part of every high school classroom, every recreational group, every social service agency. The American Friends Service Committee and all those who worked on *Bridges of Respect* deserve our gratitude for producing this timely guide.

—Margaret Hope Bacon
Philadelphia
May 1988

Contents

Introduction

This guide is presented as an invitation to adults who work with youth to recognize the needs of a neglected, largely invisible population of lesbian and gay young people. It includes a discussion of the special struggles and strengths of these youth and an extensive listing of resources—print and audiovisual materials as well as organizations, programs and projects—that will be useful to educators, health care and social service providers and youth advocates.

Gay and lesbian young people may not always be known to us, but they sit in every classroom, are members of every religious faith and denomination. Any adult who works with young people undoubtedly works with young lesbians and gays. In many instances, they are part of our families. What are we teaching them about self-worth, honesty and respect for others? When they do become known to us, how do we treat them? What do young people who are not lesbian or gay learn from us? Do they learn to hate and fear those who are different, or do they learn that differences never justify mistreatment of others?

We believe that youth workers have a responsibility to create services and programs that offer acceptance and sensitivity to all young people, including gays and lesbians. To that end, this guide also serves as an invitation to increase understanding and awareness of homophobia—the fear or hatred of lesbians and gay men—and its harmful effects on all people in our society, youth and adults alike. Homophobia is deeply ingrained in our society, on both individual and institutional levels. Even those who do not espouse homophobic views seldom recognize their destructive impact, particularly in the lives of youth.

Bridges of Respect has been developed by the Lesbian and Gay Rights Task Force of the American Friends Service Committee, a subgroup of AFSC's National Community Relations Committee. The guiding principle of the Service Committee's community relations work is "to root out those causes of injustice and violence in our society which lie in poverty and imbalance of wealth and in exclusion and denial of recognition and rights based on such factors as race, gender, class, religion, nationality, legal status and sexual orientation.'' Community relations programs touch on many diverse areas, but are "unified by a common vision of an open and non-exploitative society which recognizes the equal and infinite worth of each human being—a society in which all persons and groups are assured legal rights and in which just social and economic systems bring to all persons and groups the opportunity to live in dignity and to participate fully in the decisions affecting their lives.'' (Quoted from AFSC statement on national Community Relations work.)

The Lesbian and Gay Rights Task Force was created in 1976 to involve lesbian and gay people, along with nongay people, in addressing issues of concern to gay and lesbian communities. Over the years the Task Force has educated AFSC-related people across the country on homophobia and gay/lesbian rights, facilitated AFSC participation as a friend of the court in litigation in support of lesbian and gay rights and held a major conference, cosponsored by Philadelphia ACLU, on legal issues affecting gays and lesbians. The decision to focus now on youth issues reflects the concerns of Task Force members in their work as teachers, counselors, therapists and lawyers, as well as their personal experiences of growing up lesbian or gay.

By no means an exhaustive or definitive text, this guide may be seen as a starting point for people who want to know more about the ways in which homophobia distorts and harms the lives of young people and the adults who care for them. It explores how programs and services can be inclusive of the needs of lesbian and gay youth. It addresses the urgent need for adults to set an example of acceptance of and respect for differences among people.

In accepting this challenge, we begin the crucial work of replacing barriers of fear and silence with bridges of respect.

The listings compiled here reflect the courage and vision of people who were the first and for too long the only people to see gay and lesbian youth as full human beings, not social outcasts. With limited resources, they have made a profound and positive difference in the lives of many young people, offering genuine understanding and support. They have created a dialog of caring to help counter the emotional shocks and bruises (and sometimes the physical risks and pains) caused by homophobia.

But they are also the first to acknowledge that they alone cannot adequately do the job. Caring for youth, including those who are gay and lesbian, is a larger responsibility and must be shared by all who are engaged in the various forms of youth service. In accepting this challenge, we begin the crucial work of replacing barriers of fear and silence with bridges of respect.

ACKNOWLEDGMENTS

Completion of this project reflects the work and concern of many people, and our profound thanks go to all of them. Katharine Whitlock wrote the text and resource listings and also coordinated the massive task of reviewing hundreds of resources to select those presented here. Rachael Kamel edited the entire manuscript and in addition wrote the chapter on AIDS. Harold Jordan contributed the section on the military in the chapter on legal concerns. Jane Motz served as AFSC staff coordinator for the project. Barbara Benton was responsible for design of the guide. Florence Mabrey typed complex and repeated drafts. Sol Maria Rivera and Rachel Kelley handled correspondence.

A score of AFSC board, committee and staff members from many parts of the country helped us to identify and track down sources of information, commented on drafts of the text and helped us to think through dilemmas.

Publication of this guide was made possible in part by funding from the Chicago Resource Center and the Windom Fund.

Finally, our deep appreciation goes to those whose work on behalf of young people is reflected in the resource sections of this guide.

1 The Costs of Homophobia

"A child's personality cannot grow without self-esteem, without feelings of emotional security, without faith in the world's willingness to make room for him [or her] to live as a human being." These are the words of Lillian Smith, a civil rights activist in the 1940s. Smith urged her audiences to become aware of the ways in which behaviors and attitudes directed against particular groups (in this instance, Black people) placed so many children in jeopardy.

Basic elements necessary to our children's emotional well-being and development are denied, Smith said, when dominant groups single out others for separate and less-than-equal treatment. Healthy development, for both individuals and societies, is not possible in settings where certain children learn that they are fair game for mistreatment while others learn that it is permissible to mistreat them.

Today, homophobia—defined as the fear or hatred of lesbians and gay men—is so interwoven in our society that lesbian and gay youth face especially difficult struggles for self-esteem, emotional security and a sense of caring community. Most gay and lesbian young people are not open: they are in the closet, which is to say that they hide an important part of themselves from others (perhaps even from themselves) because they are afraid of what will happen to them if they tell the truth.

Even today it is not unusual for lesbian or gay young people never to have heard of homosexuality, to be unable to put a name to their feelings. They know only that they are "different," and that their difference is unacceptable.

A small number of young people do acknowledge their sexual orientation, at least to some important people in their lives, or are labeled by others as lesbian or gay. These identifiable youth face many of the same fears as their sisters and brothers in the closet, and they also become more obvious targets for homophobic mistreatment.

Whether in hiding or not, gay and lesbian youth know they live in a society which, in large measure, condemns them solely on the basis of their sexual orientation. Once homosexual orientation is disclosed or even suspected, it is treated as the most important thing about that young person, even though it is only one aspect of self. It is as if the young person has ceased to exist as a complete human being with the same questions, doubts and needs as heterosexual peers.

Lesbian and gay youth learn that they are seen as somehow less than human; that the quickest way to safety is to lie about themselves; that if they are found out, they will have to survive in a world that often fears and despises them.

These messages are so much a part of daily life that they go unnoticed. In schools across the country, even very young children learn the codes, passed on in joking whispers: don't wear certain colors to school on a particular day, or you're "queer." Lessons are learned each time a child discovers that one of the surest ways to deliver an insult is to accuse another of being a *lezzy*, a *faggot*, a *sissy*. Children may not always know what these words mean, but they know the pejorative power of this language; they know it is meant to belittle others.

Lessons are learned each time a homophobic joke is told and tolerated; each time adults speak and act as if everyone in the world is heterosexual, or should be.

Such manifestations of homophobia may seem inconsequential. Yet each time they go unchallenged, hostility and fear grow in their power to dominate our lives and those of our children. Possibilities for human understanding are diminished. Worse, adult acquiescence in homophobia places lesbian and gay youth at great emotional and sometimes physical risk.

What do we hear if we really start to listen? Joyce Hunter is a member of New York City's Human Rights Commission and director of social services for the Hetrick-Martin Institute for the Protection of Lesbian and Gay Youth. She tells of a male student, known to be gay, who was verbally harassed for several months by his high school gym teacher. The teacher escalated the harassment by placing the young man in a girls' gym class. The student complained to the principal, to no effect, and subsequently dropped out of school.

In another incident from the files of the Hetrick-Martin Institute, a fifteen-year-old female, who had not yet identified herself as lesbian, wrote a note to a female teacher that was interpreted by the teacher to be a love note. The student was transferred to a school for the learning disabled and mentally retarded.

Here is how one young man described his experiences to the Educational Equity Project of the Philadelphia Lesbian and Gay Task Force: "When I was in the Pearl River Middle School from sixth to eighth grade . . . I did not know I was gay. I did have a feeling I was different from everyone else. These three years were my worst years in school. I was constantly called a faggot. I did not have many friends. I was very lonely and insecure. The worst part was that I could not talk to teachers . . . about my feelings."

Perhaps one of the most bitter examples of recent years occurred in 1984, when a group of teenagers in Bangor, Maine taunted and harassed a young gay man named Charlie Howard, finally pitching him over a bridge to his death. A group of high school students in central Maine, together with one of their teachers, responded by planning a Tolerance Day program intended to spotlight the special concerns of groups who had been persecuted as minorities and to increase awareness of the human costs of intolerance. The program, including a lesbian speaker along with representatives of the Jewish, Black, Native American and other minority communities, was cancelled by the school board on the grounds that presence of a lesbian might provoke violence. The board's move was later upheld by the state Supreme Court.

School environments are not unique. Damien Martin, executive director of the Hetrick-Martin Institute, observes: "I and my coworkers have to deal every day with teenagers who have been kicked out of their homes because they are gay. We have to find a bed for the 'sissy kid' who has been raped or beaten up in the last few shelters he has gone to and who would rather risk being killed by a kinky john than going back. We have to deal with the sixteen-year-old with a temperature of 104 who would rather take his chances on disease than risk the humiliation he is used to getting from social service agencies."

Martin knows of one case where a sixteen-year-old gay youth was gang-raped in a youth shelter—and then thrown out of the shelter because the staff said "it wouldn't have happened if he wasn't gay." A seventeen-year-old wrote the Institute to tell how she had been slapped around more than once by her mother in blow-ups over her lesbianism. She moved out of her parents' home after her stepfather struck her, breaking her jaw in four places. Other young lesbians have been raped or threatened with rape when their sexual orientation became known.

Not every gay or lesbian young person experiences homophobia so violently, but all live with the risks. Moreover, such outright expressions of hostility are only the most obvious indicators of an entire atmosphere permeated with fear. Violence comes in many forms, some less tangible than physical brutality. It can be inflicted with words and actions or through silence, indifference and neglect, wounding a young person's heart and spirit.

Homophobia is so pervasive that many people do not perceive mistreatment of gay and lesbian youth as wrong. Harassment is not seen as violence, but as a "natural" response to lesbians and gays. Who cares about the hurt done to people who are not regarded as fully human?

Often, though, homophobia is expressed in overt physical violence. Across the United States, various lesbian/gay organizations gather data about the extent and varieties of homophobic violence because authorities and other institutions do not. Their efforts document that such violence is widespread and systematic, rather than a matter of isolated incidents. A 1987 survey released by the National Institute of Justice, a unit of the U.S. Justice Department, concluded that "homosexuals are probably the most frequent victims" of hate-motivated violence, but the "criminal justice system—like the rest of society—has not recognized the seriousness" of the problem.

Homophobia is so pervasive that many people do not perceive mistreatment of gay and lesbian youth as wrong. Harassment is not seen as violence, but as a "natural" response to lesbians and gays. Who cares about the hurt done to people who are not regarded as fully human?

Today, there is an increase in reports of harassment of gay/lesbian students on college campuses. The incidence of verbal or physical abuse in high schools has been and remains high. Notes the Hetrick-Martin Institute: "Much of the violence is carried out by groups of fourteen- to nineteen-year-olds and such violence is escalating sharply. Attacks by young people represent a clear failure of our schools and other social institutions to educate against violence and against homophobia."

Each time adults in positions of responsibility remain silent or look the other way when homophobic harassment occurs, children are learning that it is acceptable to tolerate violence, even to participate in it. The damage is all the worse when adults in authority actively participate in homophobic behavior.

Indifference to the destructiveness of homophobia can have another deadly, but preventable, consequence. Suicide, or attempted suicide, is one all-too-frequent choice for many lesbian/gay-identified young people who experience pain and isolation as unending; whose despair of being accepted for who they really are is almost absolute; who anticipate nothing but harm or loss—loss of family, friends—if they are honest about themselves. The Youth Suicide National Center estimates that about one in every ten teenagers attempts suicide. Recent data suggest that the rate for lesbian and gay teenagers may be dramatically higher; some studies suggest that as many as 20%-30% of lesbian/gay youth attempt suicide at least once. Many young gays and lesbians who have attempted suicide say they were afraid to tell anyone about the attempt, or about subsequent suicidal thoughts, fearing that disclosure would be met only with more rejection.

As parents, youth service providers, educators and community leaders, it is our job to ensure a safe and humane environment for all young people—and to say, through our work, that each of them matters. There are obstacles ahead, and so we must be prepared to confront the fears and stereotypes that stand in the way of constructive change.

Fears, Labels and Stereotypes

The real experiences and needs of lesbian and gay youth are shrouded in silence, obscured by the public expressions of contempt, ridicule and hostility toward homosexuals that are so commonplace in our culture. Many adults might say in all earnestness that they are unaware of the existence of sexual minority youth. Yet if this were true, why would homophobia directed toward youth be so prevalent? The problem is rather that our society offers us many labels and stereotypes but almost no information about real human beings who are gay and lesbian.

The fears giving rise to homophobic labeling are very strong, with roots far deeper than mere distaste for anyone perceived to be lesbian or gay. The emotional force of homophobic put-downs (*queer*, *sissy*, *lezzy*, *fruit*, *faggot*, *dyke*) is directed against any boy or girl, man or woman, who is judged to be stepping out of line with regard to sex role behavior. In an era like ours, when sex roles are changing for so many people, homophobia becomes a vehicle for much of the anxiety and insecurity these changes provoke.

Our society offers us many labels and stereotypes but almost no information about real human beings who are gay and lesbian.

Too many boys hide their emotions or hate themselves for having interests that could be viewed as unmanly. To call a boy a "sissy" is to tell him he's less than a man, that he's woman-like and therefore worthy of contempt or ridicule. Girls too experience the power of homophobic innuendo to intimidate females who don't conform to expected interests or behaviors.

Pre-adolescents and teenagers are particularly vulnerable to taunts that warn them they are crossing sex-role lines. Young people are in the process of discovering who they are, individually and in relation to their peers. They develop a sense of self partly by comparing themselves to others. Most want desperately to belong, to be accepted. They know that, by stepping out of line, they place themselves at great risk of being harassed and ostracized.

It takes extraordinary emotional resilience to stand up to such pressures. Some young people take the risk. A great many others are unable to resist the pressure to conform. They hide the parts of themselves that do not fit the stereotypes, developing guarded ways of relating to others, with all the incumbent emotional stress and pain. They may stifle interests or feelings that are not considered proper.

Socialization into sex roles thus forms a strong underpinning for homophobia. But there is another element as well: in the words of poet Audre Lorde, "a belief in the inherent superiority of one pattern of loving over all others and thereby its right to dominance." The name for such a belief system is *heterosexism*. Although it is often presented as an expression of "natural law" or "timeless morality," heterosexism is a social construct. Throughout history, certain groups of people have asserted superiority over others, with tragic and cruel results justified by claims of moral rectitude. Yet can any belief system be moral or ethical if it depends on hurting other people or denying whole categories of people their right to live in dignity and freedom?

Despite widespread condemnation of homosexuality as "unnatural," social scientists estimate that at least 10% of the population have a sexual orientation predominantly or exclusively towards members of the same sex. That is, for a significant number of people, homosexual orientation is as natural and deep-seated as heterosexual orientation is for others. The numbers are less important than the recognition that, while sexuality is a component of every human being, sexual orientation differs. No one knows why or how; we only know that it is so.

Sexual experiences alone do not define sexual orientation, which is, comments Damien Martin, "a fusion of sexuality and emotionality." And sexuality itself is not simply a matter of genital feelings and behaviors; it is a much deeper component of the human personality which begins developing in earliest infancy and continues to evolve into old age. Healthy sexual and emotional development go hand in hand when we are able to claim our sexuality as a beautiful, significant part of ourselves. Learning to incorporate sexuality into our lives responsibly, joyfully and with integrity should be an ongoing process, beginning in childhood. Instead, anxieties about sex often give rise to misfortunes and misunderstanding.

Homophobia serves as a magnet for many of those anxieties, especially when we address the sexuality of young people. Reluctant in many instances to forthrightly address sexuality in any terms, professionals in youth services often feel homosexuality is so charged a topic that it cannot be addressed at all. There is often an underlying fear that sexual orientation is easily influenced in children and that mere exposure to the subject (let alone role models who are gay or lesbian) is sufficient to be the determining factor. Such fears, although frequently manipulated for political purposes, are not based in fact. Moreover, they distract us from fostering healthy development of young people generally, by insisting that the gender of one's sexual partner is more important than a sense of sexual/emotional integrity.

In fact, despite prevailing beliefs, many who are lesbian or gay recognize their sexual orientation in pre-adolescent or teen years, often before any sexual involvement. Some say they always knew, even before they had a name for homosexual feelings. Others became aware of these feelings but tried to suppress them, temporarily or on into their adult years.

Young people who, in time, claim lesbianism or gayness as a part of themselves are in the process of saying who they are—first to themselves, and perhaps later to others. They are trying to name themselves. Like all youth, young gays and lesbians need to be seen in their wholeness, not reduced to labels and stigmatized. They want loving relationships with family and friends that are not dependent upon hiding, lies and disguises.

Homosexuality will continue to exist, whatever people choose to think or say about it; even the virulence of homophobia has been ineffective in preventing generations of young people from growing up with a same-sex orientation. The real issue is whether we shall begin to understand and accept the truth about human diversity, breaking down the barriers that set us apart from one another.

3 Respecting Diversity and Differences

In learning about lesbian and gay youth, it is vital to recognize that they are by no means a monolithic population, distinguished only by sexual orientation. Though they are stigmatized on that basis, there are other important facets to their lives and experiences. We are far better able to address their needs when we acknowledge and pay attention to their diversity.

For example, though there are many Black, Latino, Asian/Pacific and Native American gay and lesbian youth, the myth persists that homosexuals are predominantly white. Lesbian and gay youth of color must contend with the ways in which homophobia and racism reinforce one another. They face discriminatory treatment not only because of sexual stereotyping but also on the basis of race and culture. Few environments provide safe spaces that support healing from the pains of both forms of oppression.

Young lesbians and gays of color know that racism is as prevalent within white-dominated lesbian/gay circles as it is in the larger society. Forms of expression may be subtle or overt; one common experience is that gays and lesbians of color are admonished not to be "divisive" in predominantly white gay/lesbian settings by bringing up racial concerns. This push for "color-blindness" obscures the experiences and histories of people of color, establishing a context in which the meaning of those experiences is diminished or simply ignored.

Similarly, it is not uncommon for gay and lesbian youth of color to feel pressured to conceal or downplay their sexual orientation in families and groups that offer support for resisting the harms of racism. In our society, no racial or ethnic group is immune to homophobia.

In either case, lesbian/gay youth are pressured to choose which community they will identify with. This dichotomy is absolutely untenable for young people who need support for claiming both sexual and racial/cultural identities.

Likewise, the prevalence of sexism in both the larger society and gay/lesbian communities has ramifications for all lesbian and gay youth. For example, lesbianism receives far less public attention than male homosexuality. Yet this greater invisibility is scarcely a blessing: the implicit message is that female relationships are not particularly important, that women are not sexual beings except in relation to men. Young lesbians are resisting the tremendous social pressure on all women to center their lives around relationships to men. In later life, they will also face the economic disadvantages resulting from lack of access to a man's income. The situation may become even more complicated for young lesbians of color, who struggle with the triple jeopardy of racism, sexism and homophobia.

It is important to remember that gay and lesbian youth are part of all youth populations, without exception, whether or not they are open about their identity.

Sexism is also directly harmful to young gay males. Precisely because they are more visible, they are at especially high risk for being targets of "queer-bashing." Boys exhibiting behaviors or wearing clothing viewed as effeminate are quickly singled out for harassment.

It is beyond the scope of this guide to detail the many ways in which sexism and racism cause material and emotional damage. What matters is that it is pointless to try to establish a hierarchy of oppressions. All are wrong; all wound people. It is important for youth service providers and caregivers to help create safe spaces where lesbian/gay youth are able to feel pride and strength in being the whole people they truly are, not feeling pressured to downplay any part of themselves. It is important to remember that gay and lesbian youth are part of all youth populations, without exception, whether or not they are open about their identity.

There are other important differences among gay and lesbian youth. In rural, more geographically isolated areas, young people have even less access to a gay community than their urban peers. Teens and young adults in large cities may shy away from public exposure as much as their rural conterparts, but they have more opportunities for selective anonymity. The chance of being discovered going into a lesbian/gay bookstore or bar in a major metropolitan area, for instance, is relatively small. In rural areas and small towns, where people's lives are more closely linked, fear of exposure is particularly keen for gay and lesbian youth. Likewise, the weight of isolation is greater, since such communities are less likely to have lesbian/gay political, cultural, community service and social institutions.

Money makes a difference, too. Our society tends to blame people for their own poverty, trading in stereotypes like "white trash" or "welfare cheaters." In reality, poverty is built into our economic system; people of color, women and children are particularly at risk. For economically disadvantaged youth, many choices and opportunities are severely restricted or completely closed.

Lesbian/gay youth with physical disabilities experience all of society's biases, stereotypes and inequities toward disabled people. Chief among these is the inaccessibility of most resources, from books available only in ink-print to offices without ramps or elevators. One particularly pernicious myth is that people with disabilities are not or should not be sexual beings. Disabled youth coming to terms with sexual orientation may need particular support in affirming their sexuality.

As we go forward to create or strengthen inclusive programming, we can use our awareness to provide programs and materials that are accessible in the broadest sense of the word: to wheelchair users and to youth without money; to those who cannot read print or hear speech and to language minorities; to youth in rural areas and small towns and to those in inner cities.

We need not approach this challenge with the expectation that every effort will perfectly meet the needs of all gay and lesbian youth. Indeed, young people, like adults, sometimes need the safety and support of spaces designed for a limited range of people: only women, or only people of color, or only deaf people. At other times contexts that bring diverse groups together are of crucial importance.

What matters is being sensitive to the diversity and complexity of human experience and staying alert to opportunities to support young people for all of who they are. In the process of trying, we will learn better how to make connections, raising our own awareness and that of others. In so doing, we build bridges that we all may cross.

4 Caring Community in Personal, Social and Religious Life

Lesbian and gay youngsters face painful choices and risks. How are they to choose between honesty and possible loss of friendship or parental love? How can they fulfill their spiritual longings if they fear that their religious communities will respond with condemnation? How are they to experience such normal adolescent rituals as dating, dancing or holding hands with someone special? Even just spending time with others who are "like me" poses tremendous risks in predominantly heterosexual settings.

Some heterosexuals may find it difficult to understand how hard it is for lesbians and gay men, particularly young people, to feel at home in the world. They cannot take for granted the safety of family, religious community, youth groups or community centers. Young gays and lesbians may hide their sexuality in order to belong as much as possible, but the omnipresent anxiety and danger of being found out remain.

Many youth who have risked honesty, believing that good relationships can never be based on lies, have learned just how suddenly and powerfully things can change once their secret is revealed. Homophobic blinders may lead others—both adults and peers—to replace the young person they know and care about with images based in stereotypes and fears. In time, if people are committed to maintaining their connections with one another, they will make it through the period of estrangement. Some relationships, though, including family relationships, may be permanently ended or diminished.

Many youth who have risked honesty, believing that good relationships can never be based on lies, have learned just how suddenly and powerfully things can change once their secret is revealed.

Youth-serving professionals, no matter what their particular focus, can do much to lessen the pain of estrangement. Some major areas of need and opportunity are listed below; specific contacts are given in the resource section in the back of this guide.

1. Family support. Parents, siblings and other relatives often become hurt, frightened or confused on learning that a young person is gay or lesbian. They need aid in facing their fears, in coming to understand and accept the homosexuality of a son or daughter, sister or brother. In many parts of the country, support groups exist for parents and friends of lesbians and gays, offering peer self-help, education and emotional support.

2. Social support. Lesbian/gay young people deserve an adolescence and young adulthood that is as free as possible of fear, alienation and isolation. Providing access to such resources as pen-pal programs, rap groups and recreational/social activities (including dances) is one important way supportive adults can respond to the need of these youth for connecting with peers—with others "like me"—in nonhomophobic settings. Existing programs and models for such efforts can be used or adapted. Leaders of mixed youth groups can also work to make these groups safe for their lesbian and gay members.

3. Religious ministry. Within different faiths and many Christian denominations, efforts are underway to promote ministry that is inclusive of gay and lesbian people. The results to date are mixed; change does not come quickly or easily, and many institutions have developed theological rationales for excluding gay and lesbian people from religious community. Others treat gays and lesbians as objects of pity, in need of forgiveness or therapy. Nevertheless, there are a number of organizations and ministries serving lesbian and gay people with acceptance and respect, some with special programs or resources for youth. These include gay and lesbian congregations, both Jewish and Christian, and mixed congregations that welcome lesbian and gay members.

People of conscience hold divergent religious opinions on homosexuality and there is no universal doctrine that speaks for all. Despite the harsh condemnation of homosexuality by some religious hierarchies, a growing number of ministries are now concluding that homophobia must not stand in the way of providing spiritual community to all who seek it. Indeed, some have chosen not only to embrace lesbian and gay people at all levels of religious and spiritual life, but to take an active role in challenging homophobic discrimination.

4. Counseling. Any counseling efforts that undermine a young person's sense of self-worth will only compound the damaging effects of homophobia. It is extremely important to ensure the availability of nonhomophobic counseling services.

It is unrealistic to dismiss the problem of isolation by saying that young people who are gay and lesbian will eventually find their own way to adult gay/lesbian communities. For most of these young people, such communities seem a world away. Gay and lesbian youth need dignity, support and respect in their lives now, from the people and the communities that are important to them.

Neither does it make sense to wait for the emergence of a large visible community of lesbian/gay youth before we begin to provide all these resources. Over time, youth still in hiding will come out and sympathetic adults must be accessible to them when they do. In the meantime, the very presence of such services will send a message of acceptance to all young people and their families.

5 Providing a Safe and Equitable Educational Environment

Homophobic influences present special obstacles to educational equity for lesbian and gay students, particularly those in middle, junior high and high schools.

The first obstacle concerns ways in which the emotional and even physical safety of gay and lesbian young people is compromised. The Sexual Minority Youth Assistance League, for example, reports a situation in which a young gay male in his middle teens was continually jeered at by several teachers who used such pejoratives as *faggot* and *fruit*. They were fully aware that this boy was also being verbally and physically attacked by other students. Though he tried to seek help from other teachers and his school principal, their proposed solution was that he leave school.

The Hetrick-Martin Institute for the Protection of Lesbian and Gay Youth received this letter from another young man:

> . . . I talked to a high school counselor in confidence. But the counselor was not so discreet as I thought, and in one day the whole school found out. At first it wasn't that bad, just a little name-calling. A few weeks later, it developed into pushing around. Then the kids tried to start fights. If I know I can't defend myself against the other person, I'll run away from the problem altogether. And I did. I quit school.

A third youth wrote to the Hetrick-Martin Institute describing his experiences in a private, religiously affiliated school. Peer harassment was constant, and one instructor joined in the taunting, referring to the student in the classroom by a feminine name. The boy ran away from home several times, trying to escape from the ugliness and mean-spiritedness of his immediate world.

These examples of mistreatment by adults in positions of reponsibility are all too common. When brought to the attention of educational authorities, such incidents are frequently ignored or dismissed. Often, authorities blame the lesbian/gay students themselves for inciting attacks, a classic example of blaming the victim.

In the face of such constant homophobic abuse, it is hardly surprising that gay/lesbian youth are at high risk for truancy and dropping out. When this occurs, administrators too often ignore the damage done to the young person's educational life, believing that if the student is gone, the problem is gone. Truancy and dropping out are taken as evidence that sexual minority youth are a particularly problematic population. Yet this behavior should more properly be seen as a coping strategy, born of desperation when authorities fail to provide a safe learning environment.

A second obstacle to educational equity is found in the area of student life. School authorities have waged bitter fights against attendance by lesbian/gay couples at dances, proms and other social events and activities. When courageous young people have applied for formal recognition of gay/lesbian student organizations, their applications have often been summarily dismissed. Such actions deny to lesbian/gay groups the access to school facilities and funds enjoyed by other student groups.

Curriculum content and library resources pose a third obstacle. Finding books that present a positive view of gay and lesbian life can be very difficult for adolescents, even in large cities. If homosexuality is mentioned at all, it is typically presented with a strong homophobic bias. More absent still is any recognition of the many gay men and lesbians—of all races, cultures and faiths—who have given us works of art, examples of heroism and courage or leadership in social movements. While the contributions people make in public life are more important than any single detail of personal life, learning about the homosexual orientation of poets like Walt Whitman or Audre Lorde, novelists like Willa Cather or James Baldwin, artists like Michelangelo, human rights leaders like Bayard Rustin or Dag Hammarskjold, playwrights like Lorraine Hansberry and pioneers in social welfare like Jane Addams could help shatter homophobic stereotypes.

Homophobia is seldom explored in classroom programs focusing on other forms of oppression, such as the enslavement of Blacks in the U.S. or the Nazi Holocaust. Yet it is vitally important that young people learn that no form of intolerance arises "naturally." Prejudice has no preordained, immutable nature: it is always the result of human beliefs and actions, and it always has a traceable cultural history.

Personnel practices are a final obstacle to educational equity. Most teachers, counselors or administrators risk being fired if they are discovered to be gay or lesbian, even though legislation or executive orders in a number of communities protect employees from discrimination on the basis of sexual orientation.

Many educators remain silent in the face of homophobic harassment of their students, not because they are callous or agree with intolerance, but because they are afraid to speak up.

Within the past decade, rightwing groups have mounted several campaigns to establish legal grounds for firing not only lesbian/gay educators, but any teacher in public schools who advocates lesbian/gay rights. Though such campaigns have not succeeded to date, the very attempts have a chilling effect on educators and students alike. Needless to say, laws like these would not only codify homophobia, they would set a dangerous precedent for outlawing people because of who they are or what they believe, regardless of whatever they have or have not done.

Many educators remain silent in the face of homophobic harassment of their students, not because they are callous or agree with intolerance, but because they are afraid to speak up. They may fear creating public controversy by appearing too sympathetic to gay/lesbian young people, being accused of being gay or lesbian themselves or even losing their jobs.

Nonetheless, educators have a professional and ethical responsibility to seek a safe educational setting for all young people, regardless of differences in personal opinions about homosexuality. The paragraphs that follow sketch out the types of policy changes that would be necessary to create such a setting. Some of these suggestions could be put into practice immediately; others would require sustained campaigns by teachers, their unions, and concerned parents and community members. Helpful organizations and materials are given in the resource listings at the end of this guide.

1. Public advocacy. Creation of a good educational environment requires institutional commitment. Only a mandated effort to uproot homophobia in the schools can effect long-term, systemic change. All of us can help ensure this happens by making our views known to school boards, school superintendents, public officials, teachers' unions, professional caucuses, PTAs and school principals.

2. Enforcing responsible standards of professional and student conduct. Educators and students alike must learn that it is unacceptable to harass others, verbally or physically, and that it is also unacceptable to fail to report any instance of harassment. If such actions continue, there must be clear sanctions against the responsible individuals. Standards for appropriate conduct must be clearly stated and consistently enforced. For school personnel, placing comments about a student's sexual orientation in her or his file is an abuse of authority and another form of harassment.

3. Student activities. Policies must be developed to ensure equity for gay and lesbian students wishing to participate in student life. Such policies would prohibit discrimination in such areas as athletics, school- or student-sponsored social events and activities, membership in school-recognized or chartered clubs and organizations, chartering of groups meeting standard requirements for recognition and access to school facilities or student activity funds.

4. Faculty/staff in-service training. Mandatory training programs or workshops should be provided for the purpose of disseminating accurate information about sexual orientation, the dynamics and consequences of homophobia, diversity in the lesbian/gay population and educational equity for gay and lesbian students.

5. Employment practices. Discrimination on the basis of sexual orientation should be prohibited in matters of hiring, firing and promotion.

6. Curricula and educational resources. In such subject areas as health and sexuality/family life education, history, political science, sociology, literature and the arts, curricula should be reviewed and modified to include information about sexual orientation and people who are gay and lesbian and to integrate material on the harmful dynamics and consequences of homophobia. It is neither necessary nor desirable to censor divergent views on homosexuality; we need only ensure that school libraries and media centers include works of fiction and nonfiction containing nonhomophobic presentations of sexual orientation, as well as writings by people who are lesbian and gay.

6 Health and Sexuality Education

Social anxieties about sexuality in general are projected with special intensity onto people who are gay and lesbian and particularly onto gay and lesbian youth. Nowhere is this tendency more strongly reflected than in the treatment of homosexuality in most sex education programs and the underlying heterosexual bias in most health care services.

Whether sponsored by educational, community or religious institutions, sexuality and health programs typically censor information about homosexuality and lesbian/gay health concerns or give only cursory and inadequate attention to these topics. The subtle and none-too-subtle influence of homophobia determines what and how much will be taught.

Perhaps the most serious consequence of such imbalanced programs is seen in the panic and misinformation that surround the AIDS crisis, which is discussed in detail in the following chapter. This chapter will focus on the many other reasons for a more inclusive approach to sexuality education.

Denying accurate information about sexual orientation and human diversity fosters a great deal of unnecessary anxiety and personal anguish for young people who are gay and lesbian. At the same time, heterosexual youth receive the implied message that there are justifications for hating, fearing or ridiculing homosexually oriented people. In such an atmosphere, all youth are subtly discouraged from forming close attachments to friends of the same gender, whether or not such relationships have a homosexual dimension.

Further, this silence cuts young people off from access to preventive health care providers and diagnostic and treatment services. Lesbian and gay youth seeking gynecological/urological health care have commented on the fear they feel when asked questions about their sexual health history that presume heterosexuality. They often lie or give incomplete information, which may result in inappropriate or incomplete care, because they are terrified that disclosure of their homosexual orientation will result in humiliation and breach of confidentiality.

Silence about homosexuality also distorts perceptions of human

lives, relationships and families, leaving intact the arrogant presump-
tion that lasting and meaningful love is found only in heterosexual
bonding. This bias not only reinforces homophobic stereotypes, but
limits and hurts many young people in additional ways.

**It is easy to lose sight of the fact that sexuality is a component
of human personality that is already developing in a child's
earliest years.**

For example, young people whose parents are lesbian or gay are
frequently given the implicit message that there is something inherent-
ly wrong with the parental love and caring they receive. At times,
they are singled out for peer harassment or treated differently by
teachers—whether or not they themselves are gay or lesbian. Some
have suffered through the wrenching bitterness of prolonged legal
battles where a heterosexual parent tries to gain child custody by
charging that the other is unfit for parenthood solely because of
homosexuality.

Most young people grow up assuming that parenting is an option closed to gay men and lesbians. In fact, large numbers of lesbians and gay men are parents, and they have children in standard
ways: through childbirth or adoption. Gay and lesbian people form
loving families and committed relationships, though society neither
acknowledges nor values this reality.

Learning to make responsible decisions about health and sexuality
is one of the most important challenges facing young people. But,
as problems like teen pregnancy or the AIDS crisis illustrate, the
adult world has not been effective in providing the solid foundation of emotional and educational support they need. Fears, prejudices and denial of young people's sexuality cause us to flounder
and hesitate even in the most critical situations.

For all young people, coming to terms with oneself as a sexual
being involves far more than simplistic instruction in handling the
crisis points of sexuality: decisions about sexual involvement,
pregnancy risks and options, sexually transmitted diseases and sexual abuse or exploitation. While the crises of youth sexuality deserve
our most thoughtful and responsible attention, it is easy to lose sight
of the fact that sexuality is a component of human personality that
is already developing in a child's earliest years. Affirming the richness
of human sexuality within a context of responsibility teaches a far

greater lesson than separating youth into categories of "good" and "bad" based on their sexual decisions or orientation.

We can strengthen our commitment to comprehensive, non-homophobic, affirmative sexuality education by taking action in the areas listed below; specific contacts are given in the resource section at the end of this guide.

1. Public advocacy. Too often, organized opponents of sex education are the only voices heard by school boards and administrators. Strong coalitions of educators, parents and community groups are needed to fight for enlightened programs. This means involving parents and community leaders in program development and advocacy efforts from the beginning, wherever possible.

2. Inclusive education. Sexuality is a pleasurable and vital element of human life, and all young people, including gay and lesbian youth, deserve support for seeing it as such, while also learning about the emotional and health consequences of sexual involvement. Non-homophobic consciousness can be woven into all aspects of sexuality and family life education by removing the assumption that everyone is heterosexual and making sure that essential information is not filtered through that bias. We can educate about the harmful effects of all forms of sexual stereotyping, including homophobia.

3. Professional training and education. All professionals in youth service programs should have training opportunities for learning more about the development of human sexuality. Programs should include accurate information about sexual orientation and explore the dynamics and consequences of homophobic stereotyping, neglect and discrimination. AIDS prevention education should be mandatory.

4. Provision of health care. All youth service agencies should know how to make referrals to nonhomophobic health care providers, to those specializing in gay and lesbian health concerns and to AIDS-related programs and services. Health care providers should ensure that services and practices will be as responsive to lesbian/gay youth as to heterosexual young people. Health history forms may be modified so that heterosexuality is not presumed. Every young person should know from the beginning that s/he can depend on the maintenance of confidentiality and should receive an explanation of the importance of accurate sexual health histories.

# The AIDS Crisis

In a grim and ironic twist, the current AIDS health crisis gives us the most pointed lessons imaginable about the consequences of homophobia—while also providing an unprecedented opportunity for challenging the avoidance of such charged topics as homosexuality in sex education programs.

Recognition of homophobia is key to understanding the AIDS crisis in two distinct but related ways. First, gay youth, although they may be at higher risk for AIDS than the youth population in general, are invisible in all too many AIDS education programs and marginalized in the delivery of health and social services. As we have noted before, merely disclosing their identity can pose a considerable risk for such youth.

Second, because of the initial image of AIDS as a "gay disease," homophobia makes it more difficult to address the epidemic in clear, straightforward ways. As a result, access is limited for all young people to information and services that may be essential to their very survival.

Viruses, of course, are indiscriminate, and AIDS never was a "gay disease." Yet some people have been eager to believe so, given the early and widespread appearance of the disease (in the United States) in the gay male population. This historical accident has unalterably colored both public attitudes and official responses to this major and growing epidemic.

Racism, too, plays an important role in further hindering an effective response to the AIDS crisis. In the U.S., 25% of people with AIDS are Black and 14% are Latino—rates that are more than twice as high as the share of the population represented by these groups. Media reports and educational materials, however, have frequently masked this reality by portraying only the white experience or automatically presuming that people of color with AIDS are drug addicts.

For people of color, racism and poverty have always meant inadequate health care and services and a disproportionate toll of almost all serious diseases, not just AIDS. The spread of the AIDS epidemic through all of these neglected communities—gay, Black,

Latino—reflects, in large measure, the indifference of government institutions to these groups and years of grossly inadequate expenditures for health care, education and outreach. Only now is the funding situation beginning to improve, and many problems remain.

The most basic facts about AIDS and youth have only recently become available. Only a very small number of teens have been diagnosed with AIDS, but the figure is growing rapidly. Further, the rate is far higher among 20- to 29-year-olds. Because of the long incubation period for AIDS, averaging five years, many of these people in their twenties probably became infected in their teens.

> The spread of the AIDS epidemic through all of these neglected communities—gay, Black, Latino—reflects, in large measure, the indifference of government institutions to these groups and years of grossly inadequate expenditures for health care, education and outreach.

Millions of youth are undoubtedly engaging in activities that could place them at risk for AIDS. An estimated one in seven teenagers currently has a sexually transmitted disease. Studies of teenage women have found that well over half are sexually active, but only a few practice safer sex. Other surveys have indicated that most young people are sorely misinformed about how AIDS is transmitted and how it can be prevented. The heterosexual bias of such studies makes it impossible to derive comparable statistics for lesbian and gay youth.

Smaller but still significant numbers of youth use IV drugs, and of course needles may be shared for other purposes, such as ear-piercing or tattooing. Pregnant adolescents may risk passing the HIV virus, which causes AIDS, to their unborn children.

AIDS EDUCATION

In the absence of a vaccine or cure, preventive education is the only means at our disposal to halt the spread of AIDS, and youth are clearly an important target group for education. A turning point for such efforts came in 1986, when U.S. Surgeon General Everett Koop issued a report on AIDS. His report added a mainstream public voice to the voices of the many lesbian/gay activists, AIDS service providers (the first of whom were gay men who raised their own funds), and sexuality educators who had been calling for a massive governmental commitment to preventive education. The report included this recommendation:

> Education concerning AIDS must start at the lowest grade level possible as part of any health and hygiene program. . . . There is now no doubt that we need sex education in the schools and that it must include information on heterosexual and homosexual relationships.

Koop also called for such programs to include detailed information about the use of condoms in AIDS prevention.

An overwhelming majority of adults approve of teaching AIDS prevention through the public schools. Yet the character of such programs is a matter of bitter controversy. Some officials insist that federally funded educational materials should focus on chastity rather than explaining safer sex methods. Even more extreme are groups like the United Families Foundation, which says education programs should convey the simple message that "sex can lead to AIDS. AIDS leads to death."

In this punitive type of approach, the harmful convergence of homophobia and moralism is clearly evident. The most negative form of religious homophobia is likewise apparent in the remarks of some rightwing religious and political figures, who have termed the mounting death toll of AIDS a form of divine retribution against gays. Yet homophobia can also influence AIDS education in more subtle ways.

For example, some well-meaning educators, anxious to dispel the image of AIDS as an exclusively gay concern, have omitted all mention of gays, lesbians and homophobia from their educational materials. This approach is not only unfair to gay and lesbian youth, it also ignores the reality that, in any discussion of AIDS, attitudes and beliefs about homosexuality are part of the conversation, whether or not they are acknowledged.

As we noted at the beginning of this chapter, the AIDS crisis offers an opportunity to educators to challenge the "us-and-them" thinking which suggests that AIDS is a problem only for *other* groups of people. If educators and students alike take the opportunity to work through their own homophobia, the impact of the AIDS prevention message will be far greater.

No group of people is immune to AIDS. Indeed, the boundaries between groups like heterosexuals and homosexuals are fluid and far from absolute; they are crossed all the time. We must begin to replace the rhetoric of high-risk *groups* (which implies a false promise of being able to control the disease by segregating those groups) with an understanding of high-risk *behavior*: unsafe sexual practices, heterosexual or homosexual, and the common practice of sharing needles among people who are addicted to intravenous drugs.

Likewise, AIDS education for youth should avoid simple condemnations of sexual activity, or the life-saving message of prevention will be disregarded. Whether or not adults approve, many young people are sexually active. Sexual abstinence, affirmed as a choice, may be an empowering and self-loving option. When it is imposed as the only choice, however, the space for frank discussion is closed.

Moralistic messages about IV drug use are equally counterproductive. For young drug users, information about treatment programs or the chance to hear from a recovering addict may plant a seed of hope. It is even possible that learning how to protect one's life by sterilizing needles with chlorine bleach could spark some new thinking about the slow suicide of addiction. Injunctions from adults to avoid drug use, on the other hand, simply shut down the channels of communication.

Drug abuse is a particular menace to poor communities and communities of color—all the more so as a transmission factor in AIDS. More treatment programs and more education about AIDS prevention are urgently needed in such communities.

Some may say that a nonjudgmental stance is in itself immoral. In our view, the moral position is that no more lives should be lost to AIDS.

AIDS education is more than a matter of conveying facts; it also involves persuading people to change their behavior. Given the common belief among youth that they are personally invulnerable, this is a difficult enough task as it is. When the educational interchange is tainted with prejudice, hypocrisy and judgmentalism, the message is irretrievably lost.

In the same vein, AIDS education presented in a language or style perceived as foreign will not do its job. Educational approaches should be culturally appropriate to each community, accessible to each language minority.

Helpful resources for planning AIDS education programs are listed in the back of this guide.

TESTING AND OTHER POLICY ISSUES

The controversy over AIDS testing is another issue with considerable implications for youth. In line with the overall political climate, testing of young people for exposure to HIV (the virus that causes AIDS) has been proposed more and more widely, for example, for youth in juvenile detention, foster care or teen pregnancy programs.

The problems with this approach are many. The standard test used to detect exposure to the AIDS virus is imperfect, resulting in both false positives and false negatives. Further, the test only measures HIV exposure; it is not known whether everyone who has been exposed will go on to develop AIDS.

Another concern is whether tests are given with appropriate counseling. Cases have already been reported of youth attempting suicide after testing positive for HIV exposure. Confidentiality is another problem. Increasingly, voluntary testing programs, where confidentiality is guaranteed, are being replaced or outnumbered by mandatory or "routine" testing programs with inadequate guidelines for ensuring confidentiality of results.

Where confidentiality is not assured, those who test positive may be stigmatized and singled out for discrimination. There have been many attempts to exclude HIV-positive children and youth, or those with AIDS, from public schools. So far, all such efforts have been successfully challenged in the courts. However, proposals continue to surface to require HIV testing of youth perceived as belonging to high-risk groups before they can gain access to a variety of services. As youth advocate Abigail English observes, young people who may be at the greatest risk for AIDS—homeless or street youth, juvenile prostitutes, gay youth, young IV drug users—are precisely those youth already facing the highest risk of discrimination in the educational, legal, social welfare and health care systems.

Public health is always threatened when the health care system is used to enforce an official government definition of acceptable moral behavior. Such approaches tend to drive those at greatest risk underground, where the risk continues to multiply. Any approach to public health that prompts people to avoid the health system is clearly counterproductive.

On the other hand, some young people may wish to know their HIV status. Offered in conjunction with appropriate counseling, voluntary HIV tests can increase awareness of the AIDS crisis and encourage young people to take preventive measures. Where testing is voluntary and strictly confidential, it can have considerable value from both a public health and a personal standpoint.

Abigail English proposes two criteria for evaluating any program or policy directed to AIDS and youth. First, does it actually help prevent the spread of the AIDS virus? And second, does it counteract or promote discrimination against youth who have AIDS, test HIV-positive, or belong to perceived high-risk groups?

8 Special Needs and Social Services

As in any youth population, some young people who are gay or lesbian have histories of juvenile prostitution, drug/alcohol abuse (in themselves or their families), placement in foster care or residential care, imprisonment, dropping out of school or repeated truancy, homelessness, running away or suicide attempts. Many of them are poor, and some are considered "systems kids": that is, they may have lengthy records of involvement with the social service, mental health or prison systems.

Most of these youngsters have painful family histories, sometimes going back to infancy; many have experienced serious mistreatment and neglect. Some have been moved from one foster family or residential program to another, never knowing stability, consistency or love in their lives. Often they have learned the most negative and brutal lessons about sexuality through abuse and exploitation. Especially vulnerable to being labeled as losers and failures, they carry with them the additional pain of being singled out for mistreatment because they are lesbian or gay.

Although many agencies offer specialized services to young people with histories of neglect and abuse, few attempt to address the harm of homophobic indifference and hostility experienced by gay and lesbian youth. Worse, in many settings homophobia is still pervasive and the agency contributes to the problem. Too often the emotional difficulties and acting out behaviors of sexual minority youth are attributed to their homosexual orientation. Youth service workers may treat them as young people who *are* problems—not young people who *have* problems.

For example, one group of caseworkers, attending a workshop concerning the special needs of lesbian and gay youth, focused almost entirely on their frustrations with young gay males who cross-dressed and exhibited flamboyant or effeminate behaviors. The workers did not want to know how they could work most effectively with these young men, but only how to keep them from cross-dressing. If they could not learn that in a few quick steps, they wanted to know who else could take responsibility for the boys.

The Hetrick-Martin Institute for the Protection of Lesbian and

Gay Youth cites the example of a young man placed in a residential care facility that had a rule expressly forbidding physical and verbal violence among residents. Nevertheless, this youth was subjected to name-calling by peers. When he complained, staff informed him that, since he really was gay, use of the term *faggot* was not a violation of the rules. Finding no staff support, but facing continued harassment, the young man fought back and was subsequently expelled from residential care. Other shelters refused to accept him because he was "provocative."

Other gay youth, placed in psychiatric diagnostic or treatment centers providing short-term care, have been forced to remain long past time for transfer to residential care because no program willing to accept males labeled effeminate could be found. In still other instances, youth workers have identified excellent prospective foster parents for gay or lesbian youth, only to have those placements disallowed by their superiors. The reason: the prospective foster parents are gay or lesbian couples. Some agencies will not even consider screening lesbian or gay couples for foster parenthood; this issue has become a matter of public controversy in Massachusetts and other areas.

Too often the emotional difficulties and acting out behaviors of sexual minority youth are attributed to their homosexual orientation. Youth service workers may treat them as young people who *are* problems—not young people who *have* problems.

Even when conscientious youth workers try to respond with appropriate help or seek training that would give them specialized knowledge and skills for working with sexual minority youth, they often encounter institutional homophobic barriers. Program administrators sometimes fail to provide the leadership to ensure proper care for gay and lesbian young people because of personal homophobic attitudes. At times their failure of leadership is also the result of political or religious pressure. Too often, the needs of the young person are set aside, overridden by the desire to avoid controversy or perceptions that agency practices are "too accepting" of homosexuality.

If we look at the world through the eyes of young lesbians and gay males with histories of abuse and neglect, it is not difficult to understand their special pains and dilemmas. When they run away from abusive environments, trying to find a place where they might fit in, many end up in areas where bars, prostitution and hustling and an adult sex industry create a particular kind of street culture. It is a dangerous world but often seems less dangerous than "ordinary" life for many sexual minority youth.

Denied better environments in which to meet other gay and lesbian people, unable to find adults who do not respond with contempt and hostility, such youth may perceive the streets as their only choice. Drugs and alcohol may appear to be the best way of blotting out emotional pain; drug trafficking or prostitution may become essential for survival. The potential for sexual abuse or assault is very high in street life; even where sex is consensual, the vulnerabilities of lesbian and gay street youth make them ready targets for sexual exploitation by adult men—many of whom are heterosexual.

The objectification of people and sex so prevalent in street culture may seem horrifying. But, to young people who have known abuse and neglect most of their lives, having a sexual value of any kind may be the first time they feel they have value or power in someone's eyes.

A few pioneering programs do exist that offer a lifeline to many sexual minority youth who would otherwise become society's throwaways. These programs, and the materials available through them, are listed with the other resources in the back of this guide.

Yet this handful of programs cannot do the job alone. Among the most pressing needs in youth services are:

1. Education. Social service providers need to be well-informed about homosexuality and the special problems encountered by lesbian/gay young people. In different areas of the country, conferences for service providers have focused on the needs of sexual minority youth. Staff in-service training is also essential.

2. Prevention programs and outreach. In a number of cities, concerned individuals and organizations have created special prevention/ outreach programs designed to give gay and lesbian youth alternatives to street life and its substance abuse, hustling and bar culture. These models could be adapted to many other communities. In addition, youth service workers should be able to make referrals to agencies or individuals that can provide nonhomophobic assistance with health care, family counseling, substance abuse, job counseling, tutorial or other educational support programs, public assistance programs, emergency shelters and group homes or other residential care facilities.

3. Crisis intervention and emergency services. There is a pressing need for emergency shelter, both for those who have run away or been thrown away by their families and for young people being abused within the family because of their sexual orientation. Crisis counseling services are essential and could include hotline counseling, drop-in services, peer counseling programs or professional counseling through family service and mental health agencies.

4. Public advocacy. Long-term, systemic change will not be possible without a sustained effort to raise the consciousness of policy makers who have the power to commit the necessary resources for services to lesbian/gay youth. Political figures and religious leaders are also important. Though they may not have formal authority for controlling day-to-day operations, their help or opposition can play a critical role in determining the direction of policy.

Our long-term goal should be equity in all services for all young people who need supportive programs, including gay/lesbian youth, and creation of a nonhomophobic consciousness in all youth service delivery. But, in the short run, specialized programs for sexual minority youth may be required. Immediate needs demand attention so that the alienation and anger of gay and lesbian youth do not become further entrenched. When such programs are instituted, careful planning is necessary to minimize the possibility of creating permanent "gay ghettos" for youth, allowing mainstream services to avoid responsibility for meeting the needs of this population. Existing programs for lesbian/gay youth have given thoughtful attention to this matter and can help with strategies and tactics.

A Primer of Legal Concerns

Young people in general possess few legal rights, and even those few may not be enforceable without great emotional and financial cost. The legal situation of minors is further complicated by variations in the law in different states. Youth workers are well-advised not only to keep current on federal, state and local laws applicable to all minors, but also to recognize particular ways in which the law may touch the lives of lesbian and gay young people. (Please note that AIDS-related concerns are discussed in Chapter 7, "The AIDS Crisis.")

Sexual privacy concerns. Sodomy laws, repealed or struck down by supreme courts in a number of states and still on the books in others, generally criminalize oral and anal intercourse, even between consenting adult partners in private. While appearing to be neutral concerning sexual orientation, they are inconsistently and only sporadically enforced—almost always against gay males.

In 1986, the U.S. Supreme Court decision in *Bowers v. Hardwick* (the final vote was 5–4) upheld Georgia's sodomy law, which had been challenged by a gay man arrested in his own home. Though earlier Supreme Court rulings had affirmed a number of sexual privacy rights for adults, a majority of the court now refused to extend these protections to homosexuals. The court's decision means that states may outlaw consensual gay or lesbian sex as sodomy.

Age of consent. State laws define the age at which young people are presumed legally capable of consenting to sexual activity. They also establish age differentials used to determine whether sexual activity between a younger and an older person can legally be viewed as consensual. The intent is to prevent or penalize the sexual exploitation of young people, a legitimate and worthy purpose. However, though age-of-consent legislation is neutral with regard to sexual orientation, prosecutions and sensational media attention are more likely when a case involves two males.

Sexual and reproductive health care. Teenagers generally can seek confidential information and services from federally subsidized health care providers offering screening and treatment for sexually transmitted diseases, contraception and basic gynecological care. Agencies receiving funds under Title X of the Public Health Service Act provide services to teens without charge.

The legal status of teens with regard to abortion varies: some states require parental consent or notification before abortion services to minors are permitted; others do not. Where parental consent/ notification is required, laws generally provide a court bypass option for young people who believe informing parents will place them at risk for physical or emotional harm. Young lesbians seeking abortions may be especially concerned about the possibility of disclosure of sexual orientation, and so confidentiality is a major concern.

Military service. Lesbian and gay young adults who face a military experience are in a difficult situation. Although military enlistment policies explicitly state that "homosexuality is incompatible with military service," gay men and lesbians do serve in the military in substantial numbers. Their survival is precarious. The threat of being formally accused of homosexuality hangs over their heads constantly. It can be pulled out of the hat at any moment and used as a basis for initiating an involuntary discharge or other disciplinary action. Further, lesbian and gay service members are subjected to the most extreme forms of harassment and abuse by their peers.

Lesbian witchhunts are especially commonplace. They are often used as a way of harassing all women in the military, especially those in nontraditional jobs, regardless of their sexual orientation. Women receive discharges for "homosexuality" at more than three times the rate of men.

The military services have many ways of disciplining people accused of homosexuality. One may be subjected to intrusive and degrading investigations. Other administrative actions may be taken for which there is no recourse, such as removal of security clearances and job reassignments.

Administrative discharges are also a possibility; these may be initiated by the service member or by the government. Although administrative discharges are usually good ones, like honorable or general discharges, in recent years the services have found ways of issuing an increasing number of "other than honorable" discharges. This can happen when the military alleges that the service member has participated in homosexual activity under aggravating circumstances, which might include the use of force, coercion or intimidation, sex with someone under 16, sex in public view or on a military installation, aircraft or vessel, sex for money or sex with a subordinate. Trial by courts-martial for fraudulent enlistment (lying about sexual orientation on the enlistment forms), sodomy misconduct or other behavior considered to be discreditable to the services, although uncommon, is also a possibility.

The good news—if there is any—is that a service member who carefully prepares a request for a member-initiated homosexuality discharge is likely to receive a good discharge. It is critical that one avoid admission of specific acts, partners or incidents. Some of the organizations listed in the resources under Legal Concerns can be helpful in this area.

The AIDS crisis has added another dimension to the problems faced by gays and lesbians in the military. Testing for HIV exposure is widespread and mandatory in all service branches, including the reserve components. Under current Pentagon policies, HIV positives are not allowed to enlist. Those who turn up positive after having served in the military for a while (usually through basic and advanced training periods) can remain in the services only if they show no signs of progressive clinical illness. They will be retested regularly and restrictions placed on their assignments.

Doctor–patient confidentiality, or the lack of it, has been another serious problem. There appears to be a concerted effort by the military to circumvent restrictions imposed by Congress in 1986 on the use of statements made to medical personnel in a medical assessment and treatment context. Finally, many people with AIDS have experienced difficulties in obtaining military disability benefits.

Most disturbing is a series of recent attempts to criminalize sexual behavior for those who test HIV-positive. A number of allegedly HIV-positive service members have been court-martialed for having unsafe sex. These attempts have met with somewhat mixed results. At this writing, one major case is pending in the highest military appellate court.

A comment on the issue of gay men and the draft is in order. Theoretically gay men are exempt from the draft, but not from the draft registration requirement. It is the responsibility of the potential draftee to make known his sexual orientation if he wants to stay out of the military. Anyone contemplating such a move should be careful not to admit to any illegal acts.

Gay and lesbian youth in the service or facing the draft need very specialized assistance and counseling, in addition to personal support. The military is a separate world with its own rules and practices. The legal right to challenge military policies is severely restricted and in practice is virtually nonexistent. Young lesbians and gays in the military are forced to carry an extra burden, on top of the loss of freedom experienced by all service members and the discrimination faced by gays and lesbians in the civilian world.

School-related concerns. School boards and administrators set the policies that govern student life. Any policies or practices deemed by gay or lesbian students to deny them educational equity or to infringe on personal rights can be legally challenged, but this has usually been done on a case-by-case basis, and the outcome of any one case is by no means certain.

For example, lesbian/gay students denied formal group recognition by school authorities after meeting all standard requirements for such recognition have challenged these decisions in court. Several such challenges have been won, forcing change in publicly supported institutions. Challenges are likely to fail if the school is a privately funded religious institution.

Other lesbian and gay students have gone to court seeking the right to attend school-sponsored events, including dances and proms. At least one case, brought by a young man in New England, has proved successful.

Gay and lesbian youth may be concerned about the contents and privacy of their school records. Each school should have a written procedure for reviewing and challenging entries in school records. Students who suspect that their records contain inappropriate or irrelevant remarks about sexual orientation or other nonacademic matters may consider taking action to have such remarks removed, to prevent dissemination to colleges or prospective employers.

The case-by-case approach to securing one's right to educational equity has been useful, but challenges are costly and require tremendous emotional fortitude. Few gay and lesbian youth are able to bear the personal cost, much less the financial toll. Since most sexual minority youth are in hiding, these strategies are totally unavailable to them.

For these reasons, we may expect that sooner or later broad legal challenges will be mounted, perhaps as class action suits, calling for court-mandated remedies for the separate and less-than-equal educational status of lesbian and gay youth.

Censorship. Recently, religious fundamentalists and related political groups have mounted a particularly strong campaign to censor a wide variety of books used in classrooms and found in school libraries. A number of legal battles are currently being waged in this regard. Books targeted for censorship include works of fiction as well as nonfiction in virtually every subject area: art, history, sexuality education, political science, sociology, psychology, biology, physical sciences and more. Not only are materials with gay/lesbian themes or characters among those most frequently excluded from library shelves or classroom use, but so are many more general texts including nonhomophobic material on homosexuality.

Though we are used to taking our freedom to read for granted, that right is in peril. The Office of Intellectual Freedom of the American Library Association, People for the American Way, the American Civil Liberties Union, the Sex Information and Education Council of the U.S. and others are documenting an alarming increase in reported cases of censorship throughout the country, particularly in schools and community libraries. Young people are particularly affected by the recent Supreme Court decision that denied students the right to editorial freedom in school newspapers. Assertive legal strategies to challenge censorship are imperative.

Emancipation. Parents exercise almost complete legal control over their sons and daughters until young people have reached legal majority or are given emancipated status in the eyes of the law. Juveniles who are unhappy at home may emancipate themselves by showing the court that they fulfill certain requirements. These requirements differ from state to state, but may include age limits and showing that one has a job and place to live and can be self-sufficient. There have been a number of instances in which lesbian/gay young people, at odds with their parents in a family crisis, will move in with an older lover and attempt to emancipate themselves.

Street law. This catch-all term addresses such aspects of street life as underage drinking and bar raids, underage entry into bath houses, age-of-consent and statutory rape definitions, hustling and juvenile prostitution, runaways and so on. Because street law varies so much from state to state and city to city, those who need this knowledge may wish to seek it from juvenile justice agencies and advocates.

Time for a Change

Societal institutions are seldom pleased to have the boat rocked. Yet that is precisely what we are advocating. We are seeking to make room for lesbian and gay youth in structures permeated with homophobia. We are proposing new recognition of the dignity and worth of young people who are homosexually oriented. That is a powerful form of boat-rocking in a society that has failed to affirm the humanity of these youth, much less consider their claim to human dignity, equality and freedom.

No important struggle for broad-based social change has ever come easily, without public fear and institutional resistance. Advocates of change will find some of our efforts met with hostility and vocal opposition. We can expect to encounter homophobic personal attacks. We may be accused, directly or by innuendo, of being lesbian or gay. For those who have never experienced this, it can be a powerful opportunity for learning what gay and lesbian youth live with.

Such intimidation only works if we let it. We can counter homophobic harassment with networks of support, identifying people with whom we can honestly share our feeling and our struggles. We can also strengthen ourselves and our work by self-education, by talking with others who share our concerns and by reaching out to groups that can offer us concrete help, including many gay and lesbian community organizations.

A more subtle form of pressure comes from those who say, "I am sympathetic to your goals, but I just don't think this is the right time." The truth is, there never has been a "right time" for challenging systemic injustices and cruelties—in the eyes of institutions resistant to change. From the point of view of those who are mistreated, the time for change is always now.

The first step may be something as simple—and important—as speaking out against homophobic harassment of a young person and offering our support. Along the way, as we educate ourselves and others, we will discover that there are more people than we might have imagined who support our work and may even join in it. We will see that the young people in our lives are learning something new and better from us: a lesson about taking a stand against injustice and discovering the richness of human diversity. And we will find that we are learning from them, too, particularly from gay and lesbian youth, whose strength and courage can inspire us.

Resources

The resources listed here—both organizational programs and materials—represent the fruits of a nationwide survey and review conducted by AFSC's Lesbian and Gay Rights Task Force. In general, the criteria for inclusion were:

- Relevance to the concerns of lesbian and gay youth and adults who work with them.
- Explicit commitment to inclusiveness of lesbian/gay youth and nonhomophobic programming.
- Accessibility to others of the experiences of specialized or inclusive services.
- Sensitivity to cultural, racial, ethnic and other differences in youth populations.

This is by no means an exhaustive listing and undoubtedly some fine groups and materials have been overlooked. Both nationally and in many local communities, additional organizations exist that have an important role to play in meeting the needs of gay and lesbian youth.

The listings are generally grouped by subject area, corresponding roughly to the chapters in this book. Within each subject area, organizations and programs are given first, followed by print and audiovisual materials. Of course, many of the resources address a range of issues, and each section contains listings helpful to professionals in several areas of youth programming.

Many of the organizations listed here can provide individually negotiated consultation or training services. Every attempt has been made to ensure that these listings are accurate and appropriate for youth programming efforts; the publisher regrets any inadvertent errors or omissions. We have done our best to confirm each listing; where we were unable to obtain confirmation we have chosen to include the information anyhow for the sake of completeness.

There are several organizations, national or regional in scope, that exist exclusively to meet the needs of lesbian and gay youth and whose programs span several of the subject headings used in this guide. Each of these groups is described in detail in one or more of the sections below; in addition, they are noted here so that the breadth of their concerns will not be overlooked. Such organizations include:

- **Association of Gay and Lesbian Youth Advocates,** 2506 8th Street West, Seattle, WA 98119; (206) 282-8818. (See organizational listing under Special Needs and Social Services.)
- **Gay and Lesbian Youth Advocacy Council,** 55 Mason Street, San Francisco, CA 94102; (415) 441-4188. (See organizational listing under Special Needs and Social Services.)
- **Hetrick-Martin Institute for the Protection of Lesbian and Gay Youth,** 401 West Street, New York, NY 10010; (212) 633-8920; (212) 633-8928 TTY for the deaf. (See organizational listings under Education and Student Concerns, The AIDS Crisis and Special Needs and Social Services.)
- **National Gay Alliance of Young Adults,** P.O. Box 190426, Dallas, TX 75219-0426. (See organizational listing under Caring Community.)
- **Sexual Minority Youth Action League (SMYAL),** 1228 17th Street, NW, Washington, DC 20036; (202) 296-0221. (See organizational listing under Special Needs and Social Services.)

Homophobic Violence

ORGANIZATIONS AND PROJECTS

Anti-Violence Project
National Gay and Lesbian Task Force (NGLTF)
1517 U Street, NW
Washington, DC 20009
(202) 332-6483

The NGLTF Anti-Violence Project raises public awareness of anti-gay/lesbian violence to promote an adequate official response to the problem and to ensure adequate support services for those who are victims of violence. NGLTF has conducted violence surveys around the country and has met with representatives of a number of major official law enforcement organizations. It also distributes a variety of packets on organizing against violence and assisting victims; contact NGLTF for more information. See Print Materials listings, this section, for related publications.

Lesbian/Gay Speakers Bureau
Community United Against Violence (CUAV)
514 Castro Street
P.O. Box 14017
San Francisco, CA 94114
(415) 864-7233

Since 1978, the Lesbian/Gay Speakers Bureau of CUAV has been speaking in classrooms of the San Francisco Unified School District and Bay Area colleges. By providing students with an opportunity (often their first) to meet openly gay people, the myths, assumptions and hostilities embodied in homophobia can be openly questioned and addressed. Classroom discussions of such issues can make a positive difference for all students. The program supports CUAV's goal of minimizing and eliminating violence against gays and lesbians by targeting educational outreach to the age group that has been most likely, in the past, to commit anti-gay violence.

The program operates in compliance with a 1977 San Francisco

School Board resolution stating family life and sex education should present factual and neutral information about the lifestyles of lesbians and gay men. (For more on these policies, see Print Materials listings under Education and Student Concerns.)

PRINT MATERIALS

Anti-Gay/Lesbian Victimization: A Study by the National Gay and Lesbian Task Force and Eight Other Gay and Lesbian Organizations, National Gay and Lesbian Task Force, 1984.

Report offering one of the first in-depth analyses of the problem of violence against lesbian and gay people; includes statistics, policy recommendations and samples of the questionnaire used by participating organizations. *National Gay and Lesbian Task Force, 1517 U Street, NW, Washington, DC 20009. Single copies $5; inquire for bulk rates.*

Anti-Gay Violence, Victimization and Defamation in 1987, National Gay and Lesbian Task Force, 1987.

Examination of incidents around the country and of official responses to these incidents. *National Gay and Lesbian Task Force, 1517 U Street, NW, Washington, DC 20009. Single copies $2.*

FYI: What You Should Know About the Charlie Howard Murder, Office of Lesbian and Gay Concerns, Unitarian Universalist Association.

Information packet concerning the murder of a young gay man by a group of teenagers in Maine; powerful case illustration and analysis of homophobic violence and its implications. *Office of Lesbian and Gay Concerns, UUA, 25 Beacon Street, Boston, MA 02108. Single copies $1 postpaid.*

Caring Community in Personal, Social and Religious Life

ORGANIZATIONS AND PROJECTS: PEOPLE OF COLOR

Asian Gay Men's Support Group
P.O. Box 53074
Washington, DC 20009
(202) 234-4904

DC Asian Lesbians (DCALS)
8339 16th Street, NW, Apt. 214
Silver Spring, MD 20910
(301) 589-4462

Both groups provide support among Asian lesbians and gays. They seek to create positive attitudes, working relationships and coalitions among Asian lesbians and gays; to maintain and stress Asian culture and lesbian/gay culture; to work cooperatively with other national and local Asian organizations for civil rights; and to work cooperatively with other national and local lesbian/gay organizations. Activities include group discussions, social gatherings, educational/political outreach, consultation and training services on issues affecting Asian lesbian and gay people. Both groups are in touch with networks of Asian lesbian and gay groups nationwide; contact for local information.

Latino/a Lesbian and Gay Organization (LLEGO)
714 G Street, SE
Wasghington, DC 20003
(202) 544-0092

LLEGO is a national organization of lesbian and gay Latinas(os) established to effectively address community concerns locally, statewide, nationally and internationally. Goals include providing a forum for awareness, understanding and recognition of lesbian/gay Latino(a) unity, pride, identity, rights, relationships, alternate lifestyles and role *en nuestra comunidad*; formulating and sustain-

ing a national health agenda for the impact of AIDS, ARC, HIV +
and other health issues, developing a supportive network to facilitate
nationwide sharing of information and resources; and educating and
sensitizing individuals and communities to actively work against
issues which divide and oppress, such as sexism, racism, homophobia
and others.

National Coalition of Black Lesbians and Gays
19641 W. Seven Mile
Detroit, MI 48219
(313) 537-0484

NCBLG is the only national organization designed to address the
needs and concerns of Black lesbians and gays. Since 1978 the
organization has worked through a network of chapters and affiliate
groups and its national office to combat racial and sexual oppression through education and coalition activities with other human
and civil rights organizations. NCBLG further provides ongoing support for Black lesbians, gays and transpersons and conducts programs structured for their empowerment. NCBLG offers technical
assistance to Black lesbians, gays and transpersons in local organizing
and to existing organizations in methods of becoming racially inclusive. Inquire for membership and newsletter information.

Paz y Liberación
P.O. Box 66450
Houston, TX 77266
(713) 523-6381

PyL produces a newsletter of lesbian/gay liberation groups and
events in Latin America, Asia, Africa, the Middle East and Europe.
Covers news of the International Lesbian and Gay Youth Organization. Includes news of youth, women's and Third World groups in
the U.S. and Canada. Newsletter free to youth; to others $3/six
issues. Published approximately monthly.

PRINT MATERIALS:
PEOPLE OF COLOR

Home Girls: A Black Feminist Anthology, Barbara Smith, Ed., Kitchen Table: Women of Color Press, 1983.

Exceptional collection of writings by feminist-identified Black women, addressing, as a total work, the complex and multiple intersections of racism, sexism and heterosexism as well as issues of class and culture. Among the contributors are a number of self-identified lesbians. *Available in some libraries or through bookstores, or by mail order from Kitchen Table: Women of Color Press, P.O. Box 908, Latham, NY 12110. Single copies $11.95 paper, $20.95 cloth, plus $1 postage and handling for first book and 35 cents for each additional book.*

"Hwame, Koshkalaka, and the Rest: Lesbians in American Indian Cultures," by Paula Gunn Allen, in *The Sacred Hoop: Recovering the Feminine in American Indian Traditions,* Beacon Press, 1986.

"The lesbian is to the American Indian what the Indian is to the American—invisible." So begins Paula Gunn Allen's essay exploring lesbianism within "a larger social and spiritual tribal context." The author, a Laguna Pueblo/Sioux Indian, is a noted literary critic, author, poet and teacher of Native American Studies at the university level. *Available in some libraries or through bookstores. Single copies $10.95.*

I Am Your Sister: Black Women Organizing Across Sexualities, by Audre Lorde, Freedom Organizing Series No. 3, Kitchen Table: Women of Color Press, 1985.

Text of a moving, powerful speech by noted writer/poet/activist Audre Lorde given at the Women's Center, Medgar Evers College; Lorde speaks as a Black lesbian-feminist about heterosexism and homophobia, "two grave barriers to organizing among Black women." (10 pp.) *Kitchen Table: Women of Color Press, P.O. Box 908, Latham, NY 12110. Single copies $2.95 plus $1 postage and handling.*

In the Life: A Black Gay Anthology, Joseph Beam, Ed.,
Alyson Publications, 1986.

Powerful collection of writings by 29 Black authors exploring what
it means to be Black and gay in contemporary America. "The bot-
tom line," writes Beam, "is this: We are Black men who are proudly
gay. What we offer is our lives, our love, our visions. . . . We are
coming home with our heads held up high." Contributions organized
by sections: Stepping Out; Cut off from Among Their People;
Creating Community; Brother/Father/Lover/Son; Speaking for
Ourselves; and Stepping into Tomorrow. *Available in some libraries
or through bookstores, or by mail order from Alyson Publications,
40 Plympton Street, Boston, MA 02118. Single copies $8 plus $1
postage.*

**This Bridge Called My Back: Writings by Radical Women of
Color,** Cherríe Moraga and Gloria Anzaldía, Eds., foreword
by Toni Cade Bambara, Kitchen Table: Women of Color
Press, 1983

An anthology of writings by feminist women of color dealing with
issues of culture, class and sexuality that can divide women of col-
or; includes contributions on homophobia and heterosexism.
*Available in some libraries or through bookstores, or by mail order
from Kitchen Table: Women of Color Press, P.O. Box 908, Latham,
NY 12110. Single copies $9.95.*

"Why a Black Gay Church?" by James S. Tinney, Ph.D.,
in *In the Life: A Black Gay Anthology*, Joseph Beam, Ed., Alyson
Publications, 1986.

A compelling exploration and examination of the need for religious
ministry to Black lesbian and gay people, the exclusionary dynamics
of racism and homophobia in traditional religious life and the unique
role of Black gay ministry in creating spiritual community and serving as a catalyst for social justice. *Available in some libraries or
through bookstores, or by mail order from Alyson Publications,
40 Plympton Street, Boston, MA 02118. Single copies $8 plus $1
postage; inquire for bulk rates.*

ORGANIZATIONS AND PROJECTS: RELIGIOUS COMMUNITY

Affirmation: United Methodists for Lesbian/Gay Concerns
P.O. Box 1021
Evanston, IL 60204

Affirmation is a ministry of mutual support for lesbian and gay United Methodists and their friends and families. Local affiliates throughout the country are also involved in education and advocacy. Quarterly newsletter available by subscription for $20/year. Inquire about membership which includes newsletter. Write for affiliate locations and contacts.

Affirmation's Reconciling Congregation Program works actively with congregations seeking to promote inclusiveness of lesbians and gay men. Contact Reconciling Congregation Program, P.O. Box 24213, Nashville, TN 37202. See Print Materials listings in this section for publication.

American Baptists Concerned
872 Erie Street
Oakland, CA 94610
(415) 465-8652, 465-2778

ABC is a fellowship of gay and nongay Christians working to foster within the American Baptist Churches a community of understanding, justice and reconciliation for all, regardless of sexual orientation or affectional preference. Activities include mutual support, education and advocacy. Quarterly newsletter available at $7/year. Inquire for additional organizational information.

Brethren/Mennonite Council for Lesbian and Gay Concerns
P.O. Box 65724
Washington, DC 20035
(202) 462-2595

BMC works to provide support for Brethren and Mennonite lesbian and gay people and their parents, spouses, relatives and friends; to foster dialogue between gay and nongay people in the churches; and to provide accurate information about homosexuality from the social sciences, biblical studies and theology.

There are regional BMC groups and other informal networks

through which the work of BMC is carried forth. A newsletter is published two or three times annually and is available free to those belonging to the Mennonite or Brethren denomination and by contribution to others who would like to receive it.

Conference of Catholic Lesbians
P.O. Box 436
Planetarium Station
New York, NY 10024
(718) 353-7323

Created in 1985, the Conference is a national network of Catholic lesbians, with regional coordinators. Formation of local groups is encouraged. Biannual conference are held on Memorial Day weekend. Members receive newsletter and contact list for local areas. membership: basic $20; limited income $15; couple $25; supporting member $30 or more.

Dignity
Suite 11
1500 Massachusetts Avenue, NW
Washington, DC 20005
(202) 861-0017

Dignity is an organization of gay and lesbian Catholics and their friends. Through local chapters around the country, it provides an affirmation of one's sexual orientation within Catholic Christianity, celebrations of God's love for all persons, and resources for education within the gay/lesbian community and the wider church. Monthly newsletter available at $20/year. Write or call for further national and local information.

Friends for Lesbian and Gay Concerns
P.O. Box 222
Sumneytown, PA 18084
(215) 234-8424

FGLC is an association of lesbian, gay and nongay Friends (Quakers) who seek spiritual community within the Religious Society of Friends. Through this fellowship, women and men seek to know that of God within themselves and others and to express God's truth in both the Quaker and lesbian/gay communities as it is made clear to them. FLGC gathers twice a year, at Midwinter Gatherings and at Friends General Conferences in the summers. In addition, lesbian or gay men's gatherings and other regional gatherings are held from time to time. Quarterly newsletter by donation; $8 suggested, but any amount is acceptable.

Integrity
P.O. Box 19561
Washington, DC 20036-0561

A support group for lesbian/gay Episcopalians, their families and friends. Integrity provides fellowship, worship, education and lobbying within the Church for inclusion of lesbians and gays at all levels of spiritual life. There are local chapters throughout the United States and Canada. Inquire for more information.

The Lazarus Project
West Hollywood Presbyterian Church
7350 Sunset Boulevard
Hollywood, CA 90046
(213) 874-6646

The Lazarus Project is a ministry of reconciliation between the church and lesbians and gays inside and outside the church; an instrument of education and outreach to churches of Southern California and Hawaii encouraging dialog on sexuality and spirituality and helping to combat homophobia; a ministry encouraging the spirituality of gays and lesbians and a supportive organization to which lesbian/gay Christians already involved in the church may turn for spiritual and emotional guidance and sustenance, helping effect reconciliation with parents, families and friends. The Lazarus Project includes worship and Bible study, jail ministry, support groups, counseling, a speakers bureau and "More Light" Churches Program, conferences and various forms of educational outreach. A quarterly newsletter is available.

Lutherans Concerned/North America
P.O. Box 10461, Fort Dearborn Station
Chicago, IL 60610-0461

Lutherans Concerned, with local chapters throughout the continent, is a society of gay, lesbian and nongay Christians working to foster within Lutheran churches a climate of understanding, justice and reconciliation among all, regardless of affectional orientation. Clergy and laity from all church bodies are represented. The Reconciled-in-Christ program identifies and supports Lutheran congregations engaged in ministry inclusive of gay people. Quarterly newsletter concerning local and U.S./Canadian activities available with membership and by subscription. See Print Materials listings in this section for publication.

Ministry of Light
1000 Sir Francis Drake Blvd.
San Anselmo, CA 94690
(415) 457-1115

Ministry of Light is a non-judgmental ministry with the lesbian/gay community and with persons with AIDS/ARC; serves as a resource of support and education to individuals, families, schools, churches, synagogues, other communities of faith, and social service agencies. Services include pastoral counseling; offering of holy unions, weddings, baptisms and other celebrations of life and death; social service networking for crisis situations involving sexuality, spirituality, homophobia, heterosexism and health care; educational outreach; and more. The Rainbow's End, a program for gay, lesbian and other sexual minority youth 14-21 years of age, provides program of support, rap sessions, drop-in programs, guest speakers, social events and outreach to schools and youth agencies. Other programs of interest include AIDS Interfaith Ministry; Lesbian Mothers/Gay Fathers Support Group. A quarterly newsletter is published.

New Jewish Agenda
64 Fulton Street, No. 1100
New York, NY 10038
(212) 227-5885

With chapters in more than 40 North American cities, New Jewish Agenda works to foster traditional Jewish values of peace and social justice and to promote Jewish participation in progressive coalitions. Priority issues include feminism, Central America, the Middle East, disarmament and economic and social justice. Committed to building an inclusive Jewish community free of sexism and heterosexism, New

Jewish Agenda does ongoing educational work to combat homophobia. Agenda's "Combatting Homophobia Workshop" can help others set up community-based workshops. Inquire for more information about Agenda and its special projects. See Print Materials listing in this section for publication.

New Ways Ministry
4012 29th Street
Mt. Rainier, MD 20712
(301) 277-5674

New Ways is a ministry of reconciliation and social justice for Catholic gay/lesbian people, their families and friends and the larger Catholic and societal community. NWM seeks to provide adequate and accurate information, promote ongoing theological dialog by listening to the gay Christian experience and describe and defend human rights. Activities include workshops, seminars, counseling, production and distribution of educational resources, consultations and public speaking. Newsletter (*Bondings*) published quarterly, available for a donation. Complete list of publications available. See Print and Audiovisual listings, this section, for selected resources.

Office of Lesbian and Gay Concerns
Unitarian Universalist Association
25 Beacon Street
Boston, MA 02108
(617) 742-2100, ext. 503

This UUA office strives to eradicate homophobia and promote equality for lesbian, gay and bisexual people within the religious denomination and society through educational, programmatic and advocacy efforts. Write for a list of available publications, videocassettes and other resources, including information and referral listings. See Print Materials listings under Special Needs and Social Services and Homophobic Violence for selected resources.

Presbyterians for Lesbian/Gay Concerns
P.O. Box 38
New Brunswick, NJ 08903-0038
attn. Communications Secretary
(201) 846-1510

Presbyterians for Lesbian/Gay Concerns is an organization of ministers, elders, deacons and other members of the Presbyterian Church (U.S.A.) that strives to offer care, affirmation and support to lesbian and gay members and their families and friends; study and raise the concerns of gay and lesbian members; seek full membership and participation in the church for lesbian and gay people; encourage the mission and ministry of the Presbyterian Church with the gay/lesbian community; witness to the lesbian/gay community and to the Presbyterian Church that the church of Jesus Christ is the church for all of God's children. Monthly newsletter, *More Light Update*, with membership. Inquire for more information. More Light churches are congregations within the Presbyterian Church (U.S.A.) that have declared, through actions by their sessions, that lesbian/gay persons shall be welcomed into the family of faith as full participants. For more information about More Light ministry and churches, write to above address.

Seventh-Day Adventist Kinship International, Inc.
P.O. Box 3840
Los Angeles, CA 90078-3840
(213) 876-2076

A support group for current or former Seventh-Day Adventists who are gay men or lesbians or their friends. Activities include chapter and local meetings, Annual Kampmeeting, monthly newsletter and confidential counseling.

United Church Coalition for Lesbian/Gay Concerns
18 North College Street
Athens, OH 45701

UCCL/GC is an officially recognized special interest group within the United Church of Christ committed to ministry with and justice for lesbians and gay men and their families and friends. Chapters throughout the country sponsor a wide range of activities, including civil rights advocacy, development of religious fellowship free of homophobia and consultations on ministerial response to the AIDS health crisis and to people with AIDS. The Coalition encourages congregations to adopt "Open and Affirming" statements and policies with respect to sexual orientation, providing information and assistance to churches interested in doing so. A newsletter is published three times yearly. Inquire about additional information and complete list of available resources. See Print Materials listing in this section for pastoral care packet.

Universal Fellowship of Metropolitan Community Churches
5300 Santa Monica Boulevard, Suite 304
Los Angeles, CA 90029
(213) 464-5100

An international Christian ministry begun in response to the spiritual needs of lesbians and gay men, UFMCC includes more than 200 churches proclaiming liberation for all through a religious tradition of worship, service, social action and community. Many MCC churches offer special services, activities or programs for young people. Quarterly journal available at $8/year USA, $12 all other places. Inquire for a list of U.S./Canadian congregations or contact people. Complete catalog of publications, audio and video tapes, church materials and other resources (some available for language minorities) available from UFMCC Church Services Department at above address for $1.

Wingspan: A Ministry with and on Behalf of Gay and Lesbian People
St. Paul Reformation Lutheran Church
100 North Oxford Street
St. Paul, MN 55104
(612) 224-3371

The Wingspan ministry is directed by staff "ministry associates" working under the guidance of the church pastor and accountable to the Church Council, with the purpose of creating spiritual bridges between gay and nongay persons and communities and also between gay males and lesbians within the context of church life.

World Congress of Gay and Lesbian Jewish Organizations
P.O. Box 881272
San Francisco, CA 94188

The Congress serves as an international umbrella organization for lesbian/gay Jewish groups, primarily focusing on providing education about homosexuality within Jewish communities. Congress affiliates provide a broad spectrum of activities, based on their own needs and resources. Inquire for additional information and listings of affiliates, many of which can be valuable resources for Jewish lesbian/gay youth and their families and friends.

Many communities or regions have organizations or networks of people that can provide special ministerial support for lesbian/gay youth and their families and friends and for clergy and religious educators seeking to create inclusive ministries. Contact community or area-based lesbian and gay organizations for referrals to groups or individuals that may not be represented in the general listings provided here.

PRINT AND AUDIOVISUAL MATERIALS: RELIGIOUS COMMUNITY

And God Loves Each One: A Resource for Dialogue About the Church and Homosexuality, by Ann Thompson Cook, developed by the Dumbarton United Methodist Church Task Force on Reconciliation, 1988.

An appealing, friendly booklet providing an overview of biblical and human concerns that inevitably arise in discussions about lesbians, gay men, and the pastoral role of the church. Gentle, person-to-person approach, drawing on "real experiences of real people." Nondenominational; a good starting place for any Christian congregation. Illustrated with photographs by Joan E. Biren (JEB) and Douglas Hinckle. (20 pp., oversized pages). *Reconciling Congregation Program, P.O. Box 24213, Nashville, TN 37202. Single copies: $4.95 plus 15¢ postage/handling, prepaid. Orders of 10 or more, $3.00 per copy plus postage/handling, prepaid.*

Bibliography: The Church and Lesbian/Gay Concerns, developed by Presbyterians for Lesbian/Gay Concerns, 1987.

Annotated bibliography of print and audiovisual resources in these categories: General Works; Lesbians/Gays and the Church; Biblical/Theological Studies; Psychological/Sociological Studies; Youth and Families; Civil Rights; Pastoral Care; AIDS and Health Issues. (18 pp.) *Presbyterians for Lesbian/Gay Concerns, P.O. Box 38, New Brunswick, NJ 08903-0038. Single copies $2 postpaid.*

Breaking the Silence, Overcoming the Fear: Homophobia Education, developed by The Program Agency, Presbyterian Church (U.S.A.).

Substantive homophobia education resource publication produced following a 1984 Presbyterial Consultation, Homophobia Education: A Demonstration of Grace. Articles, essays, speeches by a broad spectrum of contributors are organized in three main subject areas: Clarifying the Problem, Biblical-Theological Perspectives, and Models for Homophobia Education. Includes resource listings for education and networking and other appendix materials. (71 pp.) *Church Education Services, Ministries with Congregations, The Program Agency, Presbyterian Church (U.S.A.), Room 1101, 475 Riverside Drive, New York, NY 10015. Single copies $3.50; inquire about bulk rates.*

A Call for Dialogue: Gay and Lesbian Christians and the Ministry of the Church, Task Force on Theology, Lutherans Concerned/North America, 1985.

Theological/pastoral issues paper. *Lutherans Concerned/North America, P.O. Box 10461, Fort Dearborn Station, Chicago, IL 60610-0461. Single copies $1.50 postpaid; inquire for bulk rates.*

Coming Out, Coming Home: Lesbian and Gay Jews and the Jewish Community, developed by New Jewish Agenda, 1987.

Welcoming lesbian and gay Jews into the Jewish community is the focus for this informative pamphlet. Topics include importance of inclusive community; understanding homophobia and heterosexism; compassionate responses to the AIDS crisis; changing attitudes within the Jewish community and suggestions for positive action. (15 pp.) *New Jewish Agenda, 64 Fulton Street, No. 1100, New York, NY 10028. Single copies 50 cents; inquire for bulk rates.*

A Conversation with Brian McNaught: On Being Gay, TRB Productions, 1986.

Award-winning author, counselor and lecturer Brian McNaught appears in this two-part, 80-minute videotape. Part 1 explores the experience of growing up gay; Part 2 examines his own youth as a gay Irish Catholic and religious intolerance toward lesbian/gay people. Beta or VHS. *New Ways Ministry, 4012 29th Street, Mt. Rainier, MD 20712. Single copy $39.50 plus $3 postage and handling.*

Keeping Posted, Vol. 32, No. 2, "Homosexuality," a periodical publication of the Union of American Hebrew Congregations, Nov. 1986.

Issue devoted to homosexuality: what Jewish tradition says about it, how modern rabbis and scholars have responded to it in the light of that tradition, and how individual Jews today have dealt with the discovery of their own homosexuality. Compassionate, caring tone; effects of public prejudice and importance of recognizing essential humanity of all gay women and men. (8 pp.) Leader's edition (teaching material) for above issue also available. *Keeping Posted, Union of American Hebrew Congregations, 838 Fifth Avenue, New York, NY 10021. Single copies $1.50; inquire for bulk rates. (Leader's edition, single copies $2.50.)*

Lesbian and Gay Liberation: A Bibliography for the Jewish Community, developed by New Jewish Agenda.

A four-page bibliography on issues important to Jewish lesbians and gay men. *New Jewish Agenda, 64 Fulton Street, No. 1100, New York, NY 10038. Single copies 30 cents; inquire for bulk rates.*

A Letter to a Friend with AIDS, Credence Cassettes, 1987.

Father Joseph Gallagher succeeds powerfully at an incredibly difficult task—bringing comfort to those facing death from AIDS. He succeeds because of the depth of his compassion and the breadth of his learning. He speaks simply and strongly, drawing on an impressive command of religious and literary sources and traditions. Inspiring and comforting. He really helps people. *Credence Cassettes, Box 414291, Kansas City, MO 64141. Single copies $7.95, multiple copies $4.95 each. Available in English and Spanish. Add $2 handling and 5% postage, or order toll-free 1-800-333-7373, MasterCard/Visa ($15 minimum), 8:00 a.m.–4:00 p.m. Central Time. Order No. AA2027 (English); AA2030 (Spanish).*

Ministry and Homosexual People, Credence Cassettes, 1981.

This five-hour program on four audio cassettes features Sister Jean-

nine Gramick, S.S.N.D. and Father Robert Nugent, S.D.S. exploring topics of special interest to those wanting to embrace lesbian/gay people in religious ministry. Topics include homosexuality, familyministry, justice and reconciliation in gay ministry, a theological overview of homosexuality, pastoral approaches, biblical witness and religious vocation. *Credence Cassettes, Box 414291, Kansas City, MO 64141. $39.95 plus $2 handling and 5% postage, or order toll-free 1-800-333-7373, MasterCard/Visa ($15 minimum), 8:00   a.m.#
4:00 p.m. Central Time. Order No. AA1419.*

More Light Ministry and Outreach, developed by Presbyterians for Lesbian/Gay Concerns.

Booklet containing information about the congregations within the Presbyterian Church (U.S.A.) that have declared through actions by their sessions that lesbian and gay persons shall be welcomed into the family of faith as full participants and that seek more light on questions of lifestyle, sexuality, loving relationships and ministry with all people. *Presbyterians for Lesbian/Gay Concerns, P.O. Box 38, New Brunswick, NJ 08903-0038. Single copies $2 postpaid.*

Open Hands, a quarterly journal from the Reconciling Congregation Program of Affirmation.

Each issue of this ministry resource has a topical focus—e.g., reconciliation, families, church policies. (See organizational listing, this section.) *Open Hands, P.O. Box 23636, Washington, DC 20006. Annual subscription $12; single issues $4 each. Write for list of back issues.*

Pastoral Care Packet, United Church Coalition for Lesbian/Gay Concerns, 1987.

A collection of biblical, theological, counseling and family life perspectives on lesbians and gay men and their families and friends; includes bibliography. *UCCL/GC, 18 North College Street, Athens, OH 45701. Single copies $7.50 postpaid.*

A Time for Dialogue.

This 52-minute video program about lesbian and gay Catholics and church ministry is divided into two parts to facilitate discussion and presents various points of view. Program includes personal faith stories of gay/lesbian Catholics, remarks by priests and women religious pioneering in ministry to homosexually oriented people,statements of bishops and dioceses on ministry to lesbian/gay people, comments on the evolving climate in Catholic theology and highlights from the historic International Dignity Convention Cathedral Eucharist. VHS or Beta. Includes program guidelines and references. *Dignity Seattle, P.O. Box 1171, Seattle, WA 98111. Checks payable to C.V.P. Services. Single copies $75 postpaid. Inquire about availability of three-quarter-inch formats.*

A Time to Speak, C. Robert Nugent, S.D.S. and Jeannine Gramick, S.S.N.D., Eds., New Ways Ministry, 1983.

Booklet containing contemporary positive perspectives on homosexuality, gay ministry and social justice from Catholic official and grassroots sources in the U.S. since 1973. Includes statements, recommendations, resolutions and editorials from Catholic bishops, newspapers, diocesan agencies, peace and justice groups, lay leaders, pastors, educators and other prominent Catholic spokespeople. *New Ways Ministry, 4012 29th Street, Mt. Rainier, MD 20712. Single copies $2 postpaid; inquire for bulk rates.*

We Are Your Children, Office of Lesbian and Gay Concerns, Unitarian Universalist Association.

A 40-minute, four-character chancel drama designed for local production, revealing the needs, concerns and struggles of lesbian and gay youth. *Office of Lesbian and Gay Concerns, UUA, 25 Beacon Street, Boston, MA 02108. Single copies $2 postpaid.*

ORGANIZATIONS AND PROJECTS: OTHER COMMUNITY GROUPS

Federation of Parents and Friends of Lesbians and Gays
(Parents FLAG)
P.O. Box 28009
Washington, DC 20038
(202) 638-3852

Parents FLAG, a national self-help, education and outreach organization with chapters in many cities and states, works toward the primary objective of helping parents and their lesbian/gay children to understand and love one another and to counteract homophobia. Activities include educational outreach and public speaking, sponsoring meetings and support groups, publishing and disseminating materials and providing parent-to-parent hotline counseling. A national newsletter provides updated information about chapter activities and projects. Write for regional telephone contacts and a list of cities where local groups exist. See Print Materials listings, this section, for selected publications.

Fund for Human Dignity, Inc.
666 Broadway, 4th Floor
New York, NY 10012
(212) 529-1600

The Fund for Human Dignity is the educational foundation of the gay and lesbian community in the United States. It is the only national organization exclusively dedicated to public education about the lives of lesbians and gay men. The Fund operates the National Gay and Lesbian Crisisline, AIDS 800, the National Gay and Lesbian Resource Center, the National AIDS Education Program, the Gay Educational Scholarships Program and the Grants Assistance Program.

Gay and Lesbian Community Services Center
Youth Department
1213 N. Highland Avenue
Los Angeles, CA 90038
(213) 464-7400

Special youth programming, provided without charge, includes young lesbian support/survival groups, special youth rap sessions, outreach and guest speakers, drug/alcohol abuse prevention programs, employment services, crisis counseling, runaway services, sports activities, social events, camping and field trips, legal aid and an STD clinic. A newsletter (*Reach*) contains information of interest to area youth. See organizational listings under Special Needs and Social Services and Education and Student Concerns for descriptions of special projects.

Gay and Lesbian Resource Center
North Central Regional Office
American Friends Service Committee
4211 Grand Avenue
Des Moines, IA 50312
(515) 277-1454

The Center provides education to service providers and the community at large in central Iowa about gay and lesbian issues, particularly regarding the needs of youth. It seeks to improve access to social services for lesbians and gays and develops support groups for lesbians and gays and their families.

Gay and Lesbian Young Adults
Dallas Gay Alliance
P.O. Box 190712
Dallas, TX 75219
(214) 528-4233
GLYA is a special interest group of the Dallas Gay Alliance, serving as a support group for gay women and men between the age of consent and 26, organized for the primary purpose of enabling gay youth to meet their peers outside of "the typical settings." GLYA activities include group discussions and rap sessions, sporting activities, and a wide variety of social events (movies, dining out, scavenger hunts, camping, a State Fair outing, etc.). GLYA is not set up to meet the special needs of youth under the age of 16; those under 18 years of age require parental consent for participation.

Gay & Lesbian Youth Association of Seattle (GLYAS)
600 East Pike, Suite 810
Seattle, WA 98122
(202) 328-5996 or 322-2777

GLYAS was formed in response to interest expressed by young people for more service, social and community education services. With elected officers and the help of an adult advisory board, this group engages in public speaking, outreach and education, outings, special projects, and fundraising. A Gay and Lesbian Youth Rap Group meets weekly, with between 20 to 40 youth attending, representing fairly equal numbers of males and females. The group is open to gay, lesbian, bisexual and concerned straight youth of ages 15-22.

Youth are welcome to invite parents. Using discussion group, role-play, panel, game and guest speaker formats, the rap group addresses a wide-ranging variety of topics including: self-esteem/self-concept; relationships; how do you know if you're gay/lesbian; dealing with homophobia at school and on the job; parent and family issues; coming out; health, AIDS, and substance abuse; careers, goals and the future; and more.

Gay Area Youth Switchboard
A Project of the Gay Youth Community Coalition of the Bay Area
P.O. Box 846
San Francisco, CA 94101-0846
(415) 386-GAYS

Run by and for gay/lesbian youth (13–25 years of age), the switchboard provides peer counseling; referrals for permanent and emergency housing, food, clothing, AIDS-related concerns, jobs and medical and mental health services; and social events and activities.

Gay/Lesbian Program
Pacific Northwest Regional Office
American Friends Service Committee
814 N.E. 40th Street
Seattle, WA 18105
(206) 632-0500

2249 E. Burnside
Portland, OR 97214
(503) 230-9427, 230-9429

This program, with staff in Portland and Seattle, works with organizations and individuals to build support and empowerment for lesbians and gay men, especially within religious communities. The program offers workshops on overcoming homophobia to churches and synagogues and other groups. Emphasis is placed on inclusion of communities of color and the issues of these communities. The program maintains a library on gay/lesbian issues. See also listing for People of Color Against AIDS Network in AIDS Crisis section.

Gay Youth Community Coalition
P.O. Box 846
San Francisco, CA 94101

The GYCC is an alliance of Bay Area lesbian/gay youth support groups and individuals pooling their efforts and resources to build a stronger young gay community. The coalition sponsors a variety of programs for youth, develops radio outreach programs and publishes a newsletter.

Lesbian and Gay Families Project
National Gay and Lesbian Task Force (NGLTF)
1517 U Street, NW
Washington, DC 20009
(202) 332-6483

The Lesbian and Gay Families Project combines the expertise of the NGLTF with the National Center for Lesbian Rights and seeks to expand the definition of "family" to encompass the family structures of lesbian and gay people so that whenever and wherever society's definition of what a family is, is applied, it is an inclusive definition. The project's three components are: education, advocacy and organizing. Information and research will be compiled and disseminated, and model legislation developed, on such issues as: foster care, adoption rights, durable powers of attorney, spousal benefits, and domestic partnership. Organizers call the Project "an important vehicle in helping us stabilize and secure family relationships within our community, another step forward in our struggle for equality and justice."

Lesbian and Gay Youth Together
c/o Minnesota Task Force for Gay and Lesbian Youth
100 North Oxford Street
Saint Paul, MN 55104
(612) 224-3371

Lesbian and Gay Youth Together is a social and support group for young people (approximate ages 15–21) who need a comfortable, safe place for getting together, exploring questions related to sexual orientation, and talking about school, family relationships, dealing with homophobia and more. Activities include guest speakers, movies, plays, potlucks and dancing. Adult advisors join to provide support and understanding.

Letter Exchange Project
Alyson Publications
40 Plympton Street
Boston, MA 02118
(617) 542-5679

Alyson Publications, a well-established gay trade publishing house offering a broad range of fiction and nonfiction titles concerning lesbian and gay youth and adults, sponsors a letter exchange to help lessen isolation among gay and lesbian teens. Guidelines for the peer correspondence program are available on request.

Minnesota Task Force for Gay and Lesbian Youth
100 North Oxford Street
Saint Paul, MN 55104
(612) 224-3371

The Task Force's mission includes providing resources and support for gay and lesbian youth, including development of peer support networks and social groups, vocational and career assistance, development of opportunities for artistic expression, access to basic needs such as food, housing and clothing, access to supportive and affirming services such as economic assistance, mental health and chemical dependency services, medical services, legal representation, assistance in handling family situations and lesbian/gay youth advocacy for health and human services professionals. Task Force membership includes professionals in religious ministry, adolescent health care, social services and mental health care.

National Federation of Parents and Friends of Gays (NF/PFOG)
820 Eastern Avenue, NW
Washington, DC 20012
(202) 726-3223

NF/PFOG is a national network of peer-counseling support groups and volunteer service providers with a special ministry and outreach to parents, families and friends of lesbians and gay men. NF/PFOG conducts workshops and seminars and distributes a wide variety of educational materials. Write (attn. Library Service) for complete publications list; see Print Materials, this section, for selected listings.

National Gay Alliance of Young Adults (NGAYA)
P.O. Box 190426
Dallas, TX 75219-0426

NGAYA was formed to help gay youth increase their understanding of themselves and to help increase the flow of information between the homosexual and heterosexual communities with regard to gay youth. Programming includes research, education and training, national project coordination and providing for positive, non-exploitative socializing opportunities. NGAYA is active in production of radio and video programming focusing on lesbian/gay youth, provides assistance in starting and sustaining local and regional gay youth/student organizations, offers a variety of print and programmatic resources and produces national profiles of gay youth via the Youthscan statistical information project. In 1986 the group sponsored the first National Gay Youth Conference, with special seminars for counselors, friends and relatives of gays. Subscription to monthly newsletter is available at $10/year. Inquire about different categories of membership, which includes newsletter. See Pen-Friend below and Print Material listings, this section, for NGAYA manual information.

National Gay and Lesbian Task Force
1517 U Street, NW
Washington, DC 20009
(202) 332-6483

The NGLTF is a gay and lesbian civil rights and public education organization. It carries out research, education, lobbying and community organizing. NGLTF conducts special projects, some of which currently focus on AIDS, anti-gay violence and public and media education.

National Gay/Lesbian Crisisline
A Project of the Fund for Human Dignity
Crisis telephone: 1-800-221-7044; NY, AK, HW: (212) 529-1604

National toll-free counseling (in continental U.S.), crisis intervention and referrals. Monday through Friday, 3:00 to 10:00 p.m., Saturday, 1:00 to 5:00 p.m. (Eastern time). For more information, contact Fund for Human Dignity, 666 Broadway, 4th Floor, New York, NY 10012; telephone: (212) 529-1600.

National Gay/Lesbian Resource Center
Fund for Human Dignity
666 Broadway, 4th Floor
New York, NY 10012
(212) 529-1600
The Resource Center collects and disseminates materials from around the country to facilitate awareness in mainstream services and programs and to help gay/lesbian communities implement or improve local programs through sharing of information and technical assistance. Inquire for complete listing of materials, prices and order form. See Print Materials listings, this section and others, for selected packets and publications.

OUTRIGHT
Portland Alliance of Gay and Lesbian Youth
P.O. Box 5025, Station A
Portland, ME 04101

OUTRIGHT is a support and social organization for gay/lesbian/bisexual young people 22 years of age and younger and meets weekly, with assistance of an adult supervisor. OUTRIGHT's community education efforts emphasize young people speaking for themselves; presentations have been given at schools, professional associations and social service agencies.

The Pacific Center for Human Growth
2712 Telegraph Avenue
Berkeley, CA 94704
(415) 841-6224

The Pacific Center is a nonprofit, professionally staffed mental health and social service agency serving lesbians, gay men, bisexuals, transvestites and transsexuals. Trained volunteers staff a lesbian/gay switchboard handling 1000 calls monthly. Educational services include community outreach; a speakers bureau offering informal talks, facilitated discussions, panel presentations, workshops and structured interviews; textbook referrals and curriculum development advisement. Individual or group counseling for both short-term and long-term needs is available. A variety of rap groups is available, including special groups for young women and young men. An AIDS education program is provided for the "worried well" and the center coordinates its AIDS efforts with other organizations and services in the Bay Area. Affirmative outreach and culturally sensitive programming for lesbians and gay men of color are an integral part of general operation.

Pen-Friend
A project of the National Gay Alliance for Young Adults (NGAYA)
P.O. Box 190426
Dallas, TX 75219-0426

Pen-Friend is a pen pal coordination service for gay adolescents and young adults, helping to lessen the isolation felt by many sexual minority youth. NGAYA notes, "In the interest of protecting our legitimate users we will not waive consideration of legal recourse against anyone who attempts to exploit this service for other than its intended use." Program guidelines are available from NGAYA.

Phoenix Rising Foundation
333 SW 5th, Suite 404
Portland, OR 97204
(503) 287-2140

The mission of the Phoenix Rising Foundation is to promote wellness in the gay and lesbian community through counseling, social/growth groups and adventure programs. Phoenix Rising offers training for mental health professionals working with lesbian/gay youth and sponsors Windfire, a social/support group for lesbian gay youth.

PRINT AND AUDIOVISUAL MATERIALS: OTHER COMMUNITY GROUPS

About Coming Out, National Gay and Lesbian Task Force, 1978.

Pamphlet exploring what "coming out of the closet" does and does not mean, its implications for the person coming out and for those in her/his life. Also available in Spanish. *National Gay/Lesbian Resource Center, Fund for Human Dignity, 666 Broadway, 4th Floor, New York, NY 10012. Checks payable to Fund for Human Dignity. Single copies 25 cents; inquire for bulk rates.*

About Our Children, Federation of Parents and Friends of
Lesbians and Gays, 8th ed., 1988.

A sensitive concise booklet inviting other parents and community
members to "help change attitudes and create an environment of
understanding so that our gay children can live with dignity and
respect." Presents factual information and shares Parents-FLAG
insights and experiences. Selected topics are translated into Chinese,
French, Japanese and Spanish. An essential resource. (15 pp.)
*Federation of Parents FLAG, P.O. Box 28009, Washington, DC
20038. Single copies $1; inquire for bulk rates.*

Answers to a Parent's Questions about Homosexuality, National
Gay and Lesbian Task Force, 1978.

Pamphlet examining a parent's most commonly asked questions and
providing concise, frank answers. *National Gay/Lesbian Resource
Center, Fund for Human Dignity, 666 Broadway, 4th Floor, New
York, NY 10012. Checks payable to Fund for Human Dignity. Single
copies 25 cents; inquire for bulk rates.*

Can We Understand?, New York City Parents FLAG, 1983.

Sensitive guide to helping parents accept, understand and talk with
gay and lesbian children. Includes religious perspectives. (16 pp.)
*National Gay/Lesbian Resource Center, Fund for Human Digni-
ty, 666 Broadway, 4th Floor, New York, NY 10012. Checks payable
to Fund for Human Dignity. Single copies 50 cents; inquire for bulk
rates.*

General Information Manual, National Gay Alliance of
Young Adults, revised 1987.

A descriptive booklet containing an in-depth discussion of NGAYA
and its pro-active, broad-based programming campaign for young
people who are homosexually oriented; includes project summaries,
an overview of the organizational structure and membership
categories and more. *NGAYA, Order Department, P.O. Box 190426,
Dallas TX 75219-0426. Single copies $3 postpaid.*

Homosexuality as Viewed from Five Perspectives, by Marcia Weitzham, Ph.D., M.F.C.C., National Federation of Parents and Friends of Gays, 1984.

Handbook providing nontechnical overviews of difficulties and problems faced by lesbians and gay men in society. Perspectives include the child, the parents, the family, the counselor and the community. (33 pp.) *NF/PFOG Resource Library, 8020 Eastern Avenue, NW, Washington, DC 20012. Single copies $2.75; inquire for bulk rates.*

Lesbian/Gay Youth Support Packet, National Gay/Lesbian Clearinghouse, Fund for Human Dignity, 1986.

Collection of materials for those exploring ways of reaching out to gay/lesbian youth. Includes media clippings, information on counseling and educational resources, program information, sample youth group flyers. *National Gay/Lesbian Resource Center, Fund for Human Dignity, 666 Broadway, 4th Floor, New York, NY 10012. Checks payable to Fund for Human Dignity. $12 per packet; inquire for bulk rates.*

Often Invisible: Counseling Gay and Lesbian Youth, Margaret S. Schneider, Ph.D., C. Psych., and Staff of the Sexual Orientation and Youth Program, Central Toronto Youth Services, Toronto, Ontario.

Book providing general information about homosexuality and a theoretical framework for examining the issues which arise when working with lesbian or gay adolescents. Topics include: adolescent development and the coming-out process; self-disclosure; lesbian/gay youth and the family; confusion and sexual orientation; multiproblem lesbian/gay youth; counseling practice; implications for social service delivery; and more. Especially useful for child care workers, social service providers, guidance counselors, correctional system workers, teachers, public health service providers, and more. *Central Toronto Youth Services, 27 Carlton Street, 3rd Floor, Toronto, Ontario, M5B IL2, Canada. Single copies: $8.50.*

One Teenager in Ten: Writings by Gay and Lesbian Youth, Ann Heron, Ed., Alyson Publications, 1983.

Anthology of writings by 28 lesbian or gay teens and young adults from throughout the U.S. and Canada. Topics include discovery of lesbian/gay feelings, deciding whether to talk honestly with friends and parents, coming out and coming to terms with being different, school experiences and religious concerns and responses. *Available in some libraries or through bookstores, or by mail order from Alyson Publications, 40 Plympton Street, Boston, MA 02118. Single copies $4 plus postage; inquire for bulk rates.*

Parents Come Out, Parents and Friends of Lesbians and Gays of San Francisco, 1985.

A highly acclaimed 28-minute video documentary of the struggle of eight parents to understand and accept their gay and lesbian children. Reflecting a spectrum of ages, races and religious backgrounds, the program moves from the earliest days after the shock of a son's or daughter's disclosure to conquering the lifelong prejudices that threatened to destroy the participants' families. Explores feelings of guilt, shame and confusion and ultimate rewards of achieving greater family closeness and honest communication. *Parents FLAG, P.O. Box 24565, Los Angeles, CA 90024. Specify VHS or Beta II format; single copies $19.95 postpaid.*

Read This Before Coming Out to Your Parents, by T. H. Sauerman, Parents and Friends of Lesbians and Gays, 1984.

Sensitively written pamphlet informing gay and lesbian young adults about the process and emotional stages most parents go through when their child's homosexual orientation is disclosed; emphasis is on "knowing what to anticipate and how to respond in a helpful manner." (15 pp.) *Federation of Parents FLAG, P.O. Box 28009, Washington, DC 20038. Single copies $1; inquire for bulk rates.*

Report on Gay and Lesbian Youth in Seattle, Seattle Commission on Children and Youth, 1989.

This is the text of a December 1988 report submitted to the Mayor and City Council of the City of Seattle by the Seattle Commission on Children and Youth. The result of a Commission effort which included a series of public hearings describes the problems and special needs of gay and lesbian youth and includes 21 recommendations for addressing them. Recommendations are included for the City, the Seattle School District, social service and health care agencies, and the media. *Seattle Commission on Children and Youth, 105 Union Street, Suite 160, Seattle, WA 98102, Inquire for availability and cost.*

Talking About School, by ·Hugh Warren (London Gay Teenage Group), 1984.

This third report of the group's research project examines the treatment of homosexuality within the school curriculum and the attitudes of teachers and educators towards issues of sexuality in general. *Available from Giovanni's Room, 1145 Pine Street, Philadelphia, PA 19107, $4.75.*

Talking About Young Lesbians, Lorraine Trenchard, Ed., (London Gay Teenage Group), 1984.

Young lesbians talk about their parents, experiences at school, relationships, men, feminism and more. *Available from Giovanni's Room, 1145 Pine Street, Philadelphia, PA 19107, $3.50.*

Why Is My Child Gay?, Federation of Parents and Friends of Lesbians and Gays, 1985.

Based on a survey of prominent scientists and researchers, this booklet presents answers from experts to the questions most commonly asked by parents and friends and by lesbians and gay people themselves, focusing on the origins of sexual orientation. *Parents FLAG, P.O. Box 27605, Central Station, Washington, DC 20038. Single copies $1; inquire for bulk rates.*

Young, Gay and Proud!, U.S. ed. edited by Sasha Alyson et al., Alyson Publications, 1985.

Candidly written book addressing such concerns as: Am I really gay? What should I tell my parents? Is it a good idea to come out in school? How can I tell if my best friend is gay? *Available in some libraries or through bookstores, or by mail order from Alyson Publications, 40 Plympton Street, Boston, MA 02118. Single copies $4 plys $1 postage; inquire for bulk rates.*

 **Education and Student Concerns**

ORGANIZATIONS AND PROJECTS

Bay Area Network of Gay and Lesbian Educators (BANGLE)
584 Castro Street, Suite 173
San Francisco, CA 94114
(415) 285-5078

BANGLE sponsors activities, including monthly support group meetings and social events, designed to help lesbians and gays in education support one another in the face of homophobia and intolerance within the educational system and society in general. A second major focus is to advocate for change in the educational system that will result in a more tolerant environment for gays and lesbians in education, whether they are students, parents, teachers or administrators. Monthly newsletter with membership.

Committee on Gay and Lesbian Youth
c/o David Solmitz
P.O. Box 346
Readfield, ME 04355

This Maine-based initiative is made up of professionals and lay people concerned with issues facing gay/lesbian youth. Through workshops and statewide conferences for professionals in education, community activists and representatives from religious communities and from the counseling professions, it strives to eradicate stereotypes, homophobia and prejudice in order to create an atmosphere of wellness for all youth.

Education Equity Project
Philadelphia Lesbian and Gay Task Force
1501 Cherry Street
Philadelphia, PA 19102
(215) 563-9584

With a team of professional educators, the PLGTF has engaged the Philadelphia School District in a dialog about the impact of homophobia in education. Continuing objectives include development and implementation of a comprehensive long-range training program for teachers, counselors and principals; development of inclusionary curriculum and the acquisition of affirmative lesbian/ gay fiction and nonfiction titles for the district's 35 public high schools.

Educational Outreach Project
Federation of Parents and Friends of Lesbians and Gays (Parents FLAG)
P.O. Box 20308
Denver, CO 80220
(303) 321-2270

In 1987 Parents FLAG mailed more than 12,000 educational packets to high school principals throughout the U.S. The packet includes a cover letter, a survey sheet and the latest edition of the booklet *About Our Children* (see Print Materials listings under Personal, Social and Religious Support). An additional 3200 packets were sent to dormitory directors and to the deans of schools of health sciences, nursing and medicine at 1600 U.S. universities, plus more than 300 to Bible colleges.

The GLEAN Project
Luke Adams, Director
c/o National Student Educational Fund
1012 14th Street, NW, Suite 207
Washington, DC 20005
(202) 347-8772

GLEAN describes itself as an educational equity and leadership development project for students and potential students identified as Gay/Bi/Lesbian, and for the professionals working with them. GLEAN will encourage and support communication, networking and information-sharing to ensure that lesbian/gay/bisexual youth are guaranteed safe schools, free of harassment. GLEAN will address public policy issues and support various activities designed to strengthen leadership development among lesbian/gay youth. This project is currently in development with the Lesbian/Bi/Gay Caucus of the United States Student Association. The National Student Educational Fund serves as USSA's educational arm.

Harvey Milk School
Hetrick-Martin Institute for the Protection of Lesbian and Gay Youth
401 West Street
New York, NY 10014
(212) 633-8920; (212) 633-8928 TTY for the deaf

Certified by the New York City Board of Education and the New York State Board of Regents, the Harvey Milk School offers a full academic and counseling program, with social service support, for lesbian and gay youth who have experienced extreme harassment in the public school system. Youth are able to obtain high school diplomas and a number of students have gone on to pursue other educational and vocational goals. The Hetrick-Martin Institute activities are highlighted in a newsletter, *Young Voices*. The Hetrick-Martin Institute pays school operating expenses, including books, supplies and rent for classroom space, in addition to providing counseling services and salaries for social workers. New York City provides a teacher.

Multicultural Lesbian and Gay Studies
300 Eshleman Hall
University of California at Berkeley
Berkeley, CA 94720
(415) 642-6942

MLGS is a student-operated program that promotes scholarly research and discussion of issues concerning lesbians and gay men. Founded in 1982 in response to the need for university courses that address these issues, MLGS sponsors classes on lesbian/gay topics and maintains a resource center to facilitate research. MLGS sponsors lectures, workshops and other educational events in cooperation with campus and community groups; the program also assists professors in integrating relevant lesbian/gay issues into existing university classes.

In concept and operations, MLGS is committed to a multicultural, multiracial approach to lesbian and gay studies. Classes, programs and materials promote awareness of the particular issues faced by lesbians and gay men of color and other groups traditionally under-represented in academia. MLGS also maintains a cosexual perspective, with equal attention to and input by lesbians and gay men. The MLGS program is a division of the Academic Affairs Office

of the Associated Students of the University of California at
Berkeley.

National Coalition of Advocates for Students (NCAS)
100 Boylston Street, Suite 737
Boston, MA 02116
(617) 357-8507

NCAS is a coalition of 24 child advocacy groups working on issues
of access and equity in the public schools. Its goal is fair and excellent public schools for all students. The organizational agenda
includes AIDS education.

Project 10
Fairfax High School
7850 Melrose Avenue
Los Angeles, CA 90046
(213) 651-5200 x24 (Virginia Uribe)

Project 10 is a unique in-school counseling program developed in
response to the unmet needs of lesbian/gay youth in the education
system. Services include emotional support, information, resources
and referral to young people who identify themselves as lesbian or
gay, or who want information on the subject. Goals include: preventing drop-out before graduation; providing campuses free of physical
violence and verbal abuse toward sexual minorities; providing intervention in alcohol and substance abuse among lesbian/gay teens;
reversing the trend of low self-esteem among lesbian/gay teenagers
by presenting positive educational images and role models; including
accurate information on lesbians and gays in educational curricula;
providing information and education about AIDS and other sexually transmissible diseases, etc.

Tutorial Program
Gay and Lesbian Community Services Center
1213 N. Highland Avenue
Los Angeles, CA 90038
(213) 464-7400, ext. 434

Volunteers from Gay and Lesbian Educators (GALE) offer one-on-one tutorials in general skills, English as a second language, resume writing, driver's license test, preparation for the GED test and any other educational services requested.

Youth and Education Committee
Illinois Gay and Lesbian Task Force
615 W. Wellington
Chicago, Illinois 60657
(312) 975-0707

The Youth and Education Committee of the Illinois Gay and Lesbian Task Force is an outreach program for counselors, teachers and others who work with adolescents. It offers a packet of information that lists resources for counselors and information on how to counsel gay and lesbian youth; provides speakers for in-service meetings; and advocates more direct, open and honest counseling to gay and lesbian youth—including necessary changes in curriculum and school programming.

PRINT MATERIALS

Board of Education Policies, developed for the San Francisco Unified School District, 1987–88.

By action of the San Francisco Board of Education, policies have been developed that may be helpful in creating a more equitable and safer educational environment for lesbian/gay youth and all young people in the San Francisco public schools. Included are Board of Education policy regarding the use of slurs, for certified personnel and also for students; notification to principals regarding implementation of the policy; and designation of individuals for counseling on human sexuality. *San Francisco Unified School District, 1950 Mission Street, San Francisco, CA 94103. Inquire attn: Administrator, Health Programs.*

Demystifying Homosexuality: A Teaching Guide About Lesbians and Gay Men, Human Rights Foundation, Irvington Publishers, 1984.

Comprehensive resource for high school teachers, counselors, parents and students, including lesson plans and classroom activities, teaching tips, question/answer section, annotated bibliography, resource list. (175 pp.) *Out of print, but may be available through local lesbian/gay organizations or libraries.*

Homophobia and Education: How to Deal with Name-Calling,
Vol. 14, Nos. 3 and 4, Interracial Books for Children Bulletin.

Special double issue with practical, informative articles on countering homophobia in the classroom, evaluating sex education literature, library materials and recommended books on gay/lesbian themes, interconnections of racism, sexism and homophobia, definitions and fact sheet and more. *Council on Interracial Books for Children, Resource Center for Educators, 1841 Broadway, Suite 500, New York, NY 10023. Single copies $3.95; inquire for bulk rates.*

Student Organization Packet, compiled by the National Gay
and Lesbian Task Force, updated 1988.

Substantive compendium of information and resources concerning campus-based lesbian/gay student organizing. Subjects include recognition; registering and funding an organization; supporting cases for student group recognition; violence on campus; organizing concerns; college nondiscrimination statements; gay studies; sample by-laws and more. Extensive resource listings of gay/lesbian student and alumni groups, national organizations, hotlines, bookstores and more. *National Gay and Lesbian Task Force, 1517 U Street, NW, Washington, DC 20009. Single copies $5.00.*

TA's Guide for Overcoming Homophobia in the Classroom, by
Alicia Abramson, developed as a joint project by the Graduate Assembly TA Training Project and the Multicultural Lesbian and Gay Studies Program, University of California at Berkeley, 1986.

Concise, useful overview of homophobia in student life/academia for teaching assistants-in-training. Includes helpful guidelines for dismantling heterosexism/homophobia in the classroom; facts about homophobia at UC. (5 pp.) *Multicultural Lesbian & Gay Studies, 300 Eshleman Hall, University of California, Berkeley, CA 94720. Inquire for availability and cost.*

# Health and Sexuality Education

See the following section for AIDS resources.

ORGANIZATIONS AND PROJECTS

National Lesbian and Gay Health Foundation
P.O. Box 65472
Washington, DC 20035
(202) 797-3708

The NLGHF was founded in 1980 as a nonprofit educational foundation, helping to coordinate information-sharing and networking systems among lesbian/gay health providers. NGLHF represents a constituency of over 20,000 health care workers with contacts throughout Canada, Australia, Europe and South America. NGLHF is committed to the creation of innovative health care programs and forums, and publishes relevant materials.

Office of Lesbian & Gay Health Concerns
New York City Department of Health
125 Worth Street, Box 67
New York, NY 10013
(212) 566-4995 (consultation & training)
(212) 691-9337 (information & referral)

The Office was established in 1983 as a formal means of linking the Department of Health to health services and providers in the lesbian and gay community on issues of concern to lesbian and gay adolescents and adults. Outreach and education services include outreach to lesbians and gay men who do not normally use existing community health resources; referrals to non-homophobic health and human service providers; community education programs; and AIDS prevention outreach for gay and bisexual men of color. Consultation and training services include "Exploring Diversity" seminars for health and social service providers; resource materials; and more. Youth needs constitute one special area of focus.

Sex Information and Education Council of the U.S. (SIECUS)
New York University
32 Washington Place
New York, NY 10003
(212) 673-3850

SIECUS is a private, nonprofit information and education organization which acts as a clearinghouse, resource center and advocate
on all aspects of sexuality, including AIDS. SIECUS offers database
searches and the Mary S. Calderon Library, the only library on all
aspects of sexuality, including AIDS, that is open to the public.
SIECUS has an extensive publications list and compiles annotated,
low-cost bibliographies on a wide variety of special topic areas, for
particular audiences, of informational and educational print and
audiovisual resources on human sexuality. Research and consultation services are available for program planning and curriculum
development. Bimonthly *SIECUS Report* available by subscription
at $40/year. Inquire about membership, which includes the *SIECUS
Report*. See Print Materials listings for selected publications.

*Many communities or regions have various organizations or agen-
cies that may be helpful in addressing the health and sexuality education needs of lesbian/gay youth and in providing training and consultation services for parents, youth and professionals. These may
include:*

- *Lesbian/gay health projects.*
- *Planned Parenthood affiliates.*
- *Feminist women's health centers.*
- *Sexuality/health/STD hotlines.*
- *STD programs.*

PRINT MATERIALS

About Sexuality and Self Respect: For Guys, Planned Parenthood
of Southeastern Pennsylvania, 1987.

A booklet written especially for males from age 12 to mid-teens,
focusing on the feelings, decisions and responsibilities associated
with sexuality and the transition from boy to man; primary theme
is the relationship between self-respect and being responsible to self

and others. Nonhomophobic, inclusive presentation. (25 pp.) *Resource Center, Planned Parenthood Southeastern Pennsylvania, 1144 Locust Street, Philadelphia, PA 19107-5740. Checks payable to PPSP. Single copies $1.25 plus 15% postage and handling; inquire for bulk rates.*

Changing Bodies, Changing Lives: A Book for Teens on Sex and Relationships, by Ruth Bell and other coauthors of *Our Bodies, Ourselves*, Random House, 1988.

Comprehensive discussion for young women and men of health, physical and emotional development, relationships and sexuality, including birth control, suicide, AIDS, food and drug abuse. Excellent factual information within the context of real lives. Section on lesbian/gay youth; discussion of harmful effects of homophobia. *Available through many bookstores and libraries. Single copies $12.95.*

Family Life/Sex Education Guidelines, adopted by the California State Board of Education, issued by the California State Department of Education, 1987.

These guidelines—not mandated, but distributed to all school districts in California—include a section on teaching about homosexuality. The section encourages teachers to present accurate information and encourages teaching respect for the dignity of the individual. Under California policy, school districts and their governing boards of education decide whether or not to implement sex education programs and, if implemented, at what level and to what extent. *California State Department of Education, P.O. Box 271, Sacramento, CA 95802-0271. Single copies $4 postpaid.*

"I think I might be a lesbian . . . now what do I do?" A Brochure for Young Women, written by Tammy, Tammi, Terryle, Camelia, Michelle, Natalie, Rebecca, and Sarah, members of OUTRIGHT, the Portland, Maine Alliance of Lesbian and Gay Youth, with help from Diane, their advisor; **"I think I might be gay . . . now what do I do?" A Brochure for Young Men,** by Kevin Cranston and Cooper Thompson, with help from members of BAGLY, Boston Area Gay and Lesbian Youth, The Campaign to End Homophobia.

Produced and distributed by The Campaign to End Homophobia, a network of people who work to end homophobia through information sharing and education, these are camera-ready pamphlets, available for reproducing with prior written permission from The Campaign, designed to provide information for lesbian/gay youth and young people questioning their sexuality. Question-and-answer format interspersed with comments from young people. Includes major national toll-free hotline listings. Inquire for prototypes and reproduction permission requests. *The Campaign to End Homophobia, P.O. Box 819, Cambridge, MA 02139.*

Sexuality . . . Decisions, Attitudes, Relationships (revised edition), Planned Parenthood Southeastern Pennsylvania, 1986.

Booklet for teens and young adults exploring personal/social aspects of sexuality. Includes sections on feelings, values formation, sex roles, sexual stereotyping, sexual orientation, sexual decision making and more. (33 pp.) *Resource Center, Planned Parenthood Southeastern Pennsylvania, 1144 Locust Street, Philadelphia, PA 19107-5740. Checks payable to PPSP. Single copies $2.50 plus 15% postage and handling; inquire for bulk rates.*

The Sourcebook on Lesbian/Gay Health Care, 2nd edition, edited by Michael Shernoff, MSW, ACSW, and William A. Scott, MSW, ACP, National Lesbian and Gay Health Foundation

Substantive compendium covering a spectrum of lesbian/gay health concerns. Articles are gathered under such subject headings as Special Populations, Mental Health, Substance Abuse, AIDS, Gay/Lesbian Families, Sexuality, and more. Narrative material is followed by special bibliographies and an annotated directory of health providers serving lesbian/gay communities. Includes discussion of listings concerning adolescent health needs. Respectful attention to diversities within lesbian/gay population. Provider directory identifies those who have Third World staff, offer languages other than English, have one or more forms of financial assistance, and/or are accessible to persons with disabilities. (425 pp.) *National Lesbian and Gay Health Foundation, Inc., P.O. Box 65472, Washington, DC 20035. Single copies $20 postpaid.*

Talking with Your Teenager: A Book for Parents, by Ruth Bell and Leni Ziegler Wildflower, Random House, 1984.

Encourages communication on all facets of parent–teen relationships; includes discussions of teen emotional well-being, sexuality and such difficult issues as substance abuse and eating disorders. Section on lesbian/gay youth concerns. *Available through bookstores or libraries.*

Winning the Battle for Sex Education, Sex Information and Education Council of the U.S. (in process of revision).

A lively and practical guide for parents and professionals who want to organize responsible, comprehensive sex education programs within their school systems; newly revised and updated version of the highly acclaimed publication is forthcoming. Includes planning and program design, strategies for developing community outreach and support and more. *SIECUS Publications, New York University, 32 Washington Place, New York, NY 10003. Write to be put on mailing list for information on price and date of availability.*

 **The AIDS Crisis**

ORGANIZATIONS AND PROJECTS

AIDS Education Program
Hetrick-Martin Institute for the Protection of Lesbian and Gay Youth
401 West Street
New York, NY 10014
(212) 633-8920; (212) 633-8928 TTY for the deaf

The AIDS Education Program is incorporated into all activities of
the Institute. It is designed to address the basic concerns of gay and
lesbian youth that may contribute to high-risk behavior, as well as
to provide basic information about AIDS, its transmission and its
prevention. The program also provides AIDS education and training for youth-serving professionals and other concerned individuals
and groups involved with youth.

AIDS Project Services
Jewish Family and Children's Services
1600 Scott Street
San Francisco, CA 94115
(415) 567-8860

Under the auspices of the Jewish Emergency Assistance Network
(J.E.A.N.), a consortium of Bay Area organizations and agencies,
Jewish Family and Children's Services offers counseling and support for people with AIDS or ARC, for their families or loved ones
and for people with other AIDS-related concerns; crisis intervention; outreach and support to out-of-town family members who lack
a local support system; community education, including a speakers
bureau on AIDS and a resource and referral service to link individuals and families in need with the total resources of the Jewish
and general communities, including pastoral counseling.

BEBASHI
(Blacks Educating Blacks About Sexual Health Issues)
1528 Walnut Street, Suite 1414
Philadelphia, PA 19102
(215) 546-4140

BEBASHI is a nonprofit coalition of health care professionals and community activists whose primary goal is providing information and education relative to sexual health in the Black community. BEBASHI's work involves community education around such issues as teenage pregnancy and control of sexually transmitted diseases. The epidemic and life-threatening nature of AIDS has made AIDs education efforts among minority people BEBASHI's current primary objective. BEBASHI provides group presentations, printed and audiovisual resource materials, media outreach, and "street education."

Family AIDS Support Project
Federation of Parents of Lesbians and Gays (PFLAG)
P.O. Box 27605
Washington, DC 20038-7605
(202) 638-4200

The Parents FLAG Task Force on Families Concerned with AIDS/ARC/HIV provides: individual family support; group support; resources for services in local communities; and updated information on national resources for people with AIDS/ARC/HIV and for their families and friends. Inquire for information about local Parents FLAG chapters.

Gay Men's Health Crisis
Box 274
132 West 24th Street
New York, NY 10011
(212) 807-7517

This pioneering AIDS organization publishes and distributes a wide variety of AIDS education/prevention information. Inquire for more information about brochures and publications available.

Latino AIDS Project
A Project of El Instituto Familiar de la Raza
2401 24th Street
San Francisco, CA 94110
(415) 647-5450

The Instituto Familiar de la Raza is a bicultural/bilingual mental health program for Latinos(as) in San Francisco; the program's philosophy is based upon the belief that La Raza population has special needs that require culturally and linguistically appropriate skills; the program seeks to reduce barriers to services and increase service effectiveness. El Instituto is also concerned with identifying the needs and barriers to services for Latinos(as) with AIDS /ARC and their families, friends and loved ones. IFR has established some unique, culturally relevant activities: a poster and mini-billboard education project to provide information on mental health, AIDs, and drug abuse; the Razathon; *El Dia de Los Muertos*; and *Las Posadas*. In addition, a Spanish-language AIDs education video was produced: *Ojos Que No Ven*. Bilingual health educators provide services for community groups, schools, churches, health fairs, employee groups and more.

National Adolescent HIV Prevention Initiative
Center for Population Options
1012 14th Street, NW., Suite 1200
Washington, DC 20005-3406
(202) 347-5700

The primary goal of CPO's intitiative is to promote the exchange of information and the development of strategies to prevent the HIV epidemic from reaching the nation's young people. Activities include: conferences bringing together educators and health care workers to share ideas, review resources and develop HIV infection prevention strategies; and publication of resource materials. CPO also conducts further research and tests innovative programs as part of its involvement with adolescents, AIDS and HIV. Inquire for more information.

National AIDS Hotline
100 Capitola Drive, Suite 202
Alston Park

Durham, NC 27713
Administrative Phone: (919) 361-4622

The National AIDS Hotline is a toll-free service available to callers 24 hours daily, seven days a week; operated by the American Social Health Association under contract with the Centers for Disease Control. Provides confidential information and referrals; information specialists available to answer personal or specific requests about AIDS and to make referrals to: public health clinics and hospitals; alternative HIV test sites; counseling and support groups; AIDS educational organizations; local hotlines; legal services. Hotline staff also arrange for mailing of free printed materials to callers through CDC-funded National AIDS Information Clearinghouse. Toll-free numbers are: TTY/TTD for Deaf Persons: (800) AIDS-TTY; Spanish Hotline: (800) 344-SIDA; English Hotline: (800) 342-AIDS.

National Military Project on AIDS
Military Law Task Force
The National Lawyers Guild
1168 Union Street, Suite 201
San Diego, CA 92101
(619) 233-1701

This project was developed in response to punitive regulations issued by the Department of Defense concerning HIV infections. MLTF has undertaken litigation for cases with precedent-setting potential and also provides other forms of legal, administrative and educational support around HIV cases. Inquire for complete listing of educational materials and prices.

National Native American AIDS Prevention Center
6239 College Avenue, Suite 201
Oakland, CA 94618
(415) 658-2051
Toll-free Hotline for all 50 states: 1-800-283-AIDS

The Center provides training and technical assistance to tribes, to Indian Health Services and to Public Health Service regarding prevention of AIDS. Offers presentations and conferences in Bay Area and on reservations. The Center provides free information packet including resource list and publishes quarterly newsletter.

Peer Education Program
Adolescent Alliance
2751 Mary Street
La Crescenta, CA 91214

The Peer Education Program on AIDS Prevention is designed to help reduce transmission of HIV in the adolescent population of Los Angeles. Multicultural teens are recruited from high schools, runaway placement centers, group homes, youth agencies and continuation schools. Following successful completion of a training program, the teen educators share AIDS prevention information in small group discussions at youth-serving organizations. Direct street outreach takes place in the beach communities of Venice and Santa Monica. The Peer program complements the Adolescent Alliance Residential Treatment Program for HIV-infected homeless teens.

People of Color Against AIDS Network
Pacific Northwest Regional Office
American Friends Service Committee
814 N.E. 40th Street
Seattle, WA 98105
(206) 632-0500

A coalition of people of color (Latino/a, Black, Native American, Asian) and minority community-based organizations providing education, information and training on AIDS as it relates to people of color. Services include training and information on special issues of youth of color and AIDS for schools and youth service organizations; training on homophobia as it relates to AIDS. A variety of resource/outreach materials have been developed. Inquire for more information.

People of Color Consortium Against Aids (POCCAA)
770 Grant Street, Suite 215
Denver, CO 80203
(303) 894-9635

A multi ethnic regional organization founded to do AIDS education among people of color who reside in communities of color in four states: Colorado, Nebraska, New Mexico and Wyoming. POCCAA's program consists or organizing regional teams of concerned agencies and individuals and involving them in outreach efforts to educate and inform their communities about AIDS. A Resource Center provides culturally sensitive materials and up-to-date data on the HIV virus. Staff are available for presentations and consultation. The Central Administrative Office and Resource Center, located in Denver, serves Colorado and Wyoming. Satellite offices are located at 243 Los Alamos Highway, Espanola, NM 87532, (505) 753-8495 and 2226 Leavenworth St., Omaha, NE 68102, (402) 341-8471.

Safe Choices Project
National Network of Runaway and Youth Services, Inc.
1400 I Street, NW, Suite 330
Washington, DC 20005
(202) 628-4114

The National Network's Safe Choices Project focuses on strengthening AIDS education and prevention efforts among member agencies working with runaway, homeless, and out of school youth, including those who are lesbian and gay. A curriculum focusing on staff training and development and on integration of AIDS education/awareness into existing services is forthcoming. Inquire for more information.

San Francisco AIDS Foundation
333 Valencia Street
Fourth Floor
San Francisco, CA 94103
Mailing address: Box 6182
San Francisco, CA 94101-6182
(415) 863-AIDS
Toll-free in Northern California: 800-FOR-AIDS
TDD (415) 864-6606

This pioneering AIDS organization publishes and distributes a wide variety of AIDS educational/prevention information. Inquire for more information about brochures and publications available and prices.

PRINT AND AUDIOVISUAL MATERIALS: EDUCATION AND PREVENTION

"Adolescents and AIDS: Legal and Ethical Questions Multiply," by Abigail English, *Youth Law News*, Vol. 8, No. 6, November-December 1987.

Insightful, clearly presented analysis of the multitude of questions concerning teenagers and AIDS. Issues include testing, confidentiality, access to services, delineation of "high-risk" status and more. *National Center for Youth Law, 1663 Mission Street, 5th Floor, San Francisco, CA 94103. Attn. editor, Youth Law News. Reprints or back issues $1.50.*

AIDS and Adolescents: Resources for Educators, developed by the Center for Population Options, 1987.

Excellent annotated listing of relevant educational resources, including curricula, pamphlets and brochures, materials for parents, movies, leader resources and ordering information. An indispensable reference. (6 pp.) *Center for Population Options, 1012 14th Street, NW, Suite 1200, Washington, DC 20005. Single copies $2.30 postpaid; inquire for bulk rates.*

AIDS and Adolescents: The Facts, developed by the Center for Population Options, 1987.

Concise two-page overview of AIDS risk in teen population. *Center for Population Options, 1012 14th Street, NW, Suite 1200, Washington, DC 20005. Single copies 42 cents postpaid; inquire for bulk rates.*

AIDS and Adolescents: The Time for Prevention Is Now, by Debra W. Haffner for the Center for Population Options, 1987.

Substantive report covering such topics as goals of AIDS prevention; AIDS prevention responsibilities for schools, religious organization, youth-serving agencies, parents and health providers; recommendations for AIDS education programs for youth; building community support and more. Excellent references, bibliography, references for additional sources of information, etc. The report was stimulated by discussions and presentations at a CPO-sposored conference on Aids and Adolescents in April 1987. (24 pp.) *Center for Population Options, 1012 14th Street, NW, Suite 1200, Washington DC 20005. Single copies $11.50 postpaid.*

AIDS and Deafness Resource Directory, The Professional & Community Training Program of the National Academy of Gallaudet University, together with the National AIDS Information Clearinghouse, 1988.

An outgrowth of the first National Conference on AIDS and Deafness, sponsored by Gallaudet University in 1988, the Directory provides access to organizations that offer AIDS-related services to deaf and hard-of-hearing people. Organizations listed alphabetically by State, and within States by city. One strength of this Directory is its careful program descriptions and detailed list of audiences served by individual organizations. (77 pp.) *National AIDS Information Clearinghouse, Department AD, P.O. Box 6003, Rockville, MD 20850 or inquire for availability through National AIDS Hotline: (800) AIDS-TTV (deaf); (800) 344-SIDA (Spanish); (800) 342-AIDS (English).*

The AIDS Crisis: Education and Policy Issues—A Statement of AFSC Understandings and Plans, developed by the American Friends Service Committee, 1987.

Guided by its Quaker belief in that of God in all peole, the AFSC's general purpose is to challenge "ourselves, our communities and governments to respect the inherent dignity of all people." This pamphlet presents AFSC's views and commitments regarding the AIDS crisis and reflects a wide AFSC consultative process. Includes Dimensions of the Crisis, Challenges to AIDS Prevention, Barriers to AIDS Prevention and Public Policy Issues, including mandatory testing and drug abuse issues. *Information Services Department, American Friends Service Committee, 1501 Cherry Street, Philadelphia, PA 19102. The first 12 copies will be sent free. Additional copies are $5/100 postpaid.*

AIDS Educator: A Catalogue of AIDS Educational Materials, developed by the San Francisco AIDS Foundation, 1988.

Includes a wide variety of resources from the San Francisco AIDS Foundation, a pioneering organization, and other groups. Selections can be made according to topic and target audience. Ordering information included. *San Francisco AIDS Foundation, Box 6182, San Francisco, CA 94101-6182.*

AIDS Fact Sheet including a Brief Guide for Pastoral Care, prepared by the Chicago Chapter of Presbyterians for Lesbian/Gay Concerns, 1987.

Basic facts about AIDS, together with discussion of ministry to persons with AIDS and ministry of reconciliation to overcome estrangement, alienation and separation resulting from homophobia. *Presbyterians for Lesbian/Gay Concerns, c/o Communications Secretary, P.O. Box 38, New Brunswick, NJ 08903-0038. Inquire for price.*

Criteria for Evaluating an AIDS Curriculum, developed by the National Coalition of Advocates for Students, 1987.

Available in both English and Spanish editions, this publication is intended for use by parents, teachers, school administrators and students in developing effective AIDS education programs. Designed primarily for school-based programs, it is also appropriate for youth-serving agencies. Includes a chart matching student developmental stages at various grade levels with appropriate approaches to AIDS education. *National Coalition of Advocates for Students, 100 Boylston Street, Suite 737, Boston, MA 02116. Single copies $2 postpaid. Specify English or Spanish edition.*

Educational Materials Catalogue and Order Form, American College Health Association, 1988.

Tha American College Health Association, a professional association through which institutions of post-secondary education and individuals, both health professionals and students, relate to the health needs of academic communities, publishes a health information series of pamphlets. Titles include Women & AIDS; AIDS: What Everyone Should Know; The HIV Antibody Test; Safer Sex; and more. Series emphasizes awareness, risk reduction and prevention for young adults. Inquire for information. *American College Health Association, 15879 Crabbs Branch Way, Rockville, MD 20855.*

Family Support Guide, Federation of Parents FLAG, 1989.

The Guide is a packet which includes material on HIV infection; infection precautions; emotional support for people coping with illness and death; current technical information on medical treatments, drug trials and alternative treatment options; and home care instructions. *Federation of Parents and Friends of Lesbians and Gays, P.O. Box 27605, Washington, DC 20038-7605. Single copies $5.*

Focus: A Review of AIDS Research, a monthly publication of the AIDS Health Project, University of California at San Francisco.

AIDS research information is appearing quickly, in almost staggering amounts. It is the goal of *Focus* to place the data and medical reports in a context that is meaningful and useful to its readers. An excellent source of understandable information for health care and human service providers, educators and others; for example, February 1987 issue included such articles as "Educating Youth About AIDS," and "Ethnic and Racial Misconceptions About AIDS." *Subscriptions for 12 monthly issues at $24 for California residents outside the San Francisco Bay Area, $30 for other U.S. residents and $42 in other countries. Checks payable to U.C. Regents. Subscription requests to: Focus, UCSF AIDS Health Project, Box 0884, San Francisco, CA 94143-0884. Inquire for back issues at same address or telephone (415) 476-6430.*

How to Talk to Your Children About AIDS, developed by Sex Information and Education Council of the U.S. (SIECUS) and School of Education, Health, Nursing and Arts Professions, New York University, 1986.

Brochure includes basic facts about AIDS, guidelines for discussing AIDS with children, and special suggestions for addressing children at different developmental/age levels. *SIECUS, 32 Washington Place, New York, NY 10003. Single copy free with stamped, self-addressed business-size envelope. Additional copies up to 50, 60 cents each. Inquire for larger bulk quantities and rates.*

A Letter to a Friend with AIDS, Credence Cassettes, 1987.

See listing under Caring Community.

Se Met Ko, developed by Haitian Women's Program, New York Metropolitan Regional Office, American Friends Service Committee, 1989.

A lively 28-minute educational video (also available on film) in Haitian Creole with English subtitles, by and for the Haitian community. Culturally specific but broadly accessible, Se Met Ko presents Haitian characters who empower themselves, taking action to prevent the spread of HIV infection. Accompanying discussion guide in Creole and English. *Haitian Women's Program, AFSC, 15 Rutherford Place, New York, NY 10003. Purshace $160; 2 week rental $30. Also available in ¾ inch and 16 mm; inquire for prices (212) 598-0965.*

Surgeon General's Report on Acquired Immune Deficiency Syndrome, C. Everett Koop, M.D., Sc.D., Surgeon General of the U.S. Public Health Service, U.S. Department of Health and Human Services, 1986.

Concise report on AIDS "to the people of the United States," providing straightforward information on AIDS, how it is transmitted, relative risks of infection and how to prevent it. Includes discussion of future areas of concern, including recommendations for prevention education. Informational resource listings. (36 pp.) *Available in English or Spanish edition. Free in any quantity. Call toll-free 1-800-342-7514.*

Teaching AIDS: A Resource Guide On Acquired Immune Deficiency Syndrome, by Marcia Quackenbush and Pamela Sargent, Network Publications, revised 1988.

A practical, refreshingly flexible and stimulating guide for providing AIDS education to teenagers and young adults. Applicable to a variety of educational settings. Subjects include basic facts about AIDS; safe and unsafe sexual activities; teaching plans that address AIDS in a variety of contexts, including medical, civil rights, public health and more; teaching materials and worksheets. Some useful background materials, including special tips for teachers. (163 pp.) *Network Publications, P.O. Box 1830, Santa Cruz, CA 95061-1830. Single copies $19.95 plus 15% postage and handling.*

PRINT MATERIALS: CIVIL LIBERTIES, PUBLIC POLICY AND LEGAL ISSUES

ACLU of Northern California Policy on AIDS and Civil Liberties, Civil Liberties Union of Northern California, 1986.

Newsprint edition of ACLU-NC policy on AIDS, antibody testing, quarantine, surveillance and compulsory tracing, drug laws, public schools, right to treatment, insurance, prisons and the military. *ACLU-NC, 1663 Mission Street, Suite 460, San Francisco, CA 94103. Single copies free; inquire for bulk rates.*

AIDS and Your Legal Rights, National Gay Rights Advocates, 1986.

Brochure in NGRA's Consumer Education Series; succinct review for general readers of major legal concerns and issues. (8 pp.) *National Gay Rights Advocates, 540 Castro Street, San Francisco, CA 94114. Single copies $2; inquire for bulk rates.*

AIDS: Basic Documents, Lesbian and Gay Rights Project, American Civil Liberties Union, 1987.

Collection of basic legal/medical articles that help answer questions most often asked about AIDS, public health and civil rights. *Lesbian and Gay Rights Project, American Civil Liberties Union, 132 West 43rd Street, New York, NY 10036. $5 each.*

AIDS Legal Guide: A Professional Resource on AIDS-Related Issues and Discrimination, Lambda Legal Defense and Education Fund, 1987 (second edition).

Comprehensive guide on legal dimensions and implications of AIDS, for lawyers, gay rights advocates and others. (100 pp.) *Lambda Legal Defense and Education Fund, 132 West 43rd Street, New York, NY 10036. Single copies postpaid, $15/individuals and $25/institutions; inquire about bulk rates.*

AIDS Practice Manual, National Gay Rights Advocates and National Lawyers Guild, 1987 (second edition).

Substantive legal and educational guide for attorneys dealing with AIDS-related legal concerns and discrimination. *National Gay Rights Advocates, 540 Castro Street, San Francisco, CA 94114. $35 for* non-members, $25 for members.

AIDS Testing in the Military—A Handy Guide: The Facts, Your Rights, Citizen Soldier.

6-panel brochure explaining the legal and medical issues raised by the armed forces' mandatory HIV-antibody testing. Citizen Soldier, a nonprofit GI and veterans rights group, distributes a copy free to those who write and request the pamphlet and also sponsors radio public service announcements concerning the brochure, featuring actor Edward Asner. *Citizen Soldier, 175 Fifth Avenue, New York, NY 10010.*

AIDS Update.

A succinct, comprehensive monthly newsletter covering nationwide litigation, legislation and advocacy concerning AIDS and AIDS-related discrimination. *Lambda Legal Defense and Education Fund, 666 Broadway, New York, NY 10012. Annual subscription for 11 monthly issues: $30 for Lambda members, $50 for non-members, $75 for institutions.*

Are You In the Military? Are You Worried About the AIDS Test?, developed by the National Military Project on AIDS, Military Law Task Force, National Lawyers Guild.

Single-page handout summarizing implications of mandatory HIV testing in armed forces, designed especially for active duty personnel. Simple, clear, concise. *Military Law Task Force, National Lawyers Guild, 1168 Union Street, No. 201, San Diego, CA 92101. Single copies 25 cents each; inquire for bulk rates.*

What the ACLU Has to Say About AIDS and Civil Liberties, American Civil Liberties Union, 1987.

Leaflet outlining the ACLU's response to frequently asked questions about AIDS, including antibody testing, reporting of test results, job discrimination and more, for classroom and general educational use. *American Civil Liberties Union, Literature Department, 132 West 43rd Street, New York, NY 10036. Single copies free; inquire about bulk rates.*

 # Special Needs and Social Services

Organizations and Projects

The Association of Gay and Lesbian Youth Advocates
2506 8th West
Seattle, WA 98119
(206) 282-8818

It is the purpose of AGLYA to protect the interests of gay and lesbian youth, to prevent their exploitation, to promote their physical and mental well-being, to identify the specific and special needs of this population, to educate the general public in appropriate agencies and other concerned groups about these needs and to encourage, promote and monitor the delivery of appropriate services to these young people. To these ends, AGLYA serves as a referral service, providing information for street youth and runaways and a directory of discussion and support groups for youth, friends and families. It provides educational resources through a library of up-to-date video and print materials and offers workshops and presentations for youth, families, teachers and counselors, led by qualified professionals in the fields of education, medicine and the social services.

Case Management and Consultation Services
Hetrick-Martin Institute for the Protection of Lesbian and Gay Youth
401 West Street
New York, NY 10014
(212) 663-8920; (212) 633-8928 TTY for the deaf

The Hetrick-Martin Institute works with individual youth, their families and social service agencies with specific or general problems dealing with gay and lesbian youth. Whenever possible, this program refers clients to existing services. Priorities are collaboration with other agencies and consistency of caring response. Where the client is referred to another agency, the Institute monitors the client's course through that agency.

Education and Training Services
Hetrick-Martin Institute for the Protection of Lesbian and Gay Youth
401 West Street
New York, NY 10014
(212) 633-8920; (212) 633-8928 TTY for the deaf

Educators from the Institute provide information on issues facing
lesbian and gay youth and their families to a variety of professional
audiences, including educators and social service providers, and to
school-age youth and young adults. Curricula prepared by professional educators and clinicians include basic information about
homosexuality and bisexuality; social, emotional and physical health
issues facing lesbian and gay youth and their families; AIDS education and prevention and problems confronting service providers.
Special programs provide training in counseling and intervention
strategies appropriate to this client population. The Institute also
offers an annual conference open to all professionals who work with
youth.

Emergency Services Program
Gay and Lesbian Community Services Center
1213 North Highland Avenue
Los Angeles, CA 90038
(213) 464-7400

The goal of this program is to develop a stabilizing life plan addressing the future vocational and residential needs of clients. The
program provides crisis intervention, housing for males and females
on an emergency basis (15–30 days) and transitional living quarters
(up to 60 days) for those between the ages of 18 and 23. The program also provides life skills training, roommate referral services,
clothing for all ages, food vouchers for clients, assistance in obtaining birth certificates and ID cards, phone service for employment purposes, medical and legal referrals and bus tokens for job
interviews and other appointments. Ongoing counseling, health and
vocational needs are referred to the appropriate center programs
or other agencies.

Equity Institute
Tucker-Taft Building
48 N. Pleasant Street

Amherst, MA 01002
(413) 256-0271
The Institute works with schools, churches, government agencies, businesses and social change organizations, providing training, curricula, technical assistance and written and audiovisual materials that focus on affirming diversity. Issues include race, sex and age discrimination, sexual harassment, heterosexism, classism and anti-Semitism. Services include Appreciating Diversity Program (heterosexism/homophobia program for public educators). Newsletter free of charge to members, $25/year for non-members. Inquire about other publications and curriculum materials.

Ethnic and Sexual Minority Youth Suicide Conference
c/o San Francisco Delinquency Prevention Commission
170 Fell Street, No. 21
San Francisco, CA 94102
(415) 554-7630

In March, 1988, a pioneering conference on the "hidden victims" of youth suicide—ethnic and sexual minority youth—focused on the invisibility, nature and causes of suicide and suicidal ideation in these groups. Sponsored by a diversity of youth-serving organizations and endorsed by many more, the project serves as an example of ways community organizations can address special, pressing needs of neglected youth.

Gay and Lesbian Adolescent Social Services, Inc. (GLASS)
8235 Santa Monica Blvd. #214
West Hollywood, CA 90046

GLASS provides two fully staffed, state licensed homes for gay and lesbian youth; a third facility is planned. Also offered: programs where carefully screened adult volunteers become friends and role models for gay and lesbian youth; AIDS educaton and prevention programs that take information to the streets; a Foster Family Project to help caring gay/lesbian adults become foster parents; and a sexual abuse prevention program providing gay and lesbian youth with the information and encouragement they need to help protect themselves. A mobile outreach unit may be added which will travel the streets, providing food, clothing and information to any gay or lesbian youngster in need.

Gay and Lesbian Youth Advocacy Council
55 Mason Street
San Francisco, CA 94102
att'n Hank Wilson
(415) 441-4188

GLYAC advocates for gay and lesbian youth in such areas as social services, mental health, criminal justice, and the like. Special emphasis is placed on educational advocacy at the local, state and national levels. GLYAC is also involved in youth suicide prevention efforts, locally, statewide and nationally.

Hetrick-Martin Institute for the Protection of Lesbian and Gay Youth
401 West Street
New York, NY 10014
(212) 633-8920; (212) 633-8928 TTY for the deaf

The Hetrick-Martin Institute is a not-for-profit organization working to protect the interests of lesbian and gay youth, to prevent their exploitation and to promote their mental and physical well-being. Specific goals include educating the public, youth-serving agencies and other concerned groups about the needs of lesbian and gay youth; promoting and monitoring appropriate services to these youth; promoting coordination of existing services; retaining youth in their biological, foster or adoptive homes wherever possible; preventing delinquency and encouraging research about lesbian and gay youth.

Free and confidential services include rap groups, individual and family therapy, educational counseling, tutoring and G.E.D. preparation, job and vocational training assistance, social activities, recreation programs, AIDS education programs for youth and youth-serving professionals, a street outreach program for homeless youth and juvenile prostitutes and emergency information on shelter, food, clothing, medical attention and legal advice. The institute also works to fill the void that currently exists in demographic data about lesbian and gay adolescents, by conducting needs surveys in all program areas. Several research projects that have been completed are available to agencies upon request. Inquire about copies of testimony presented to various government bodies concerning specific educational, health and social service needs of lesbian and gay youth. See additional Hetrick-Martin Institute program listings in this section and under Education and Student Concerns and The AIDS Crisis.

Larkin Street Youth Center
Larkin Street Services
1044 Larkin Street
San Francisco, CA 94109
(415) 673-0911

Established to serve homeless and runaway youth (heterosexual, gay, lesbian and bisexual) from all ethnic and class backgrounds, Larkin Street provides "a backdrop to turn around young lives caught in . . . a downhill spiral. We help these runaway and homeless kids reconstruct their dreams by providing a safe place for change where love and caring abound." Professional staff and trained volunteers provide street outreach; counseling services; a drop-in center for rapping and recreation; basic medical services; education, tutoring and some basic skills training; AIDS education; referrals for shelter, emergency clothing, and food; After Care program for those 18-21 years of age who continue to live on the streets; substance abuse education and support for recovery. Where possible, the program helps to reunite young people with their families.

The National Network of Runaway and Youth Services
1400 I Street, NW, Suite 330
Washington, DC 20005
(202) 682-4114

The National Network is dedicated to developing the capacity of the U.S. to broaden the personal, social, economic, educational and legal options and resources available to runaway and homeless youth and other at-risk youth and their families and communities. The Network gathers data, monitors legislation and policy decisions affecting at-risk youth and disseminates information through publications, conferences and media outreach.

The Network is sensitive to and supportive of efforts to responsibly and adequately meet the needs of lesbian and gay youth; seePrint Materials listings under Education and Student Concerns for publication. Inquire for more information about Network membership, special programs and projects, publications, and training and support services.

Offstreets
A Project of Minneapolis Youth Division
1637 Hennepin Avenue
Minneapolis, MN 55403
(612) 338-3103

Offstreets, a drop-in center serving males and females ages 12–18, provides a safe, comfortable atmosphere where young people can meet with counselors and learn about helping resources. Intended to meet the special needs of street youth, including lesbian and gay young people, it provides counseling, food, emergency shelter, clothing, medical referrals, recreational activities, informational groups and employment referrals.

Seattle Youth and Community Services
1020 Virginia
Seattle, WA 98101
(206) 622-3187

SYCS provides long-term and emergency services to runaway, homeless and street youth. The group is also involved in legislative advocacy for displaced youth and strives to increase knowledge about displaced youth in order to improve service delivery. Within this context, SYCS includes services to gay- and lesbian-identified youth, such as emergency and short-term housing and long-term foster care (in gay/lesbian homes), meals, medical services, educational services, employment services, drug and alcohol counseling, AIDS education (including a safe sex support group) and individual and family counseling. SYCS also sponsors an ongoing street youth theater project. Staff are available for consultation or training in recruiting and licensing gay/lesbian foster homes and developing programs on gay/lesbian street youth, adolescent prostitution and more.

Sexual Minority Youth Action League (SMYAL)
1228 17th Street, NW
Washington, DC 20036
(202) 296-0221

SMYAL is a youth service/advocacy agency, working to counter the abuse, neglect and self-hatred of young people in the Washington, DC metropolitan area who are gay, lesbian, bisexual, transsexual or transvestite. Activities include direct services to youth and their families, case consultation with other youth service agencies, training and education for adult youth workers, weekly socialization group for young men and women 14–21 years of age, telephone information and referral, public policy advocacy and general community education.

SMYAL can provide a bibliography of books and journal articles on sexual minority youth issues; $1 donation requested. SMYAL also publishes a quarterly newsletter, with each issue including a background paper on a specific topic (e.g., suicide, addiction, adolescent sexual development); sample issue free. Subscription free with memberships; individuals $20/year, nonprofit organizations $50, businesses and government agencies $75. Video library maintained; inquire for list and availability.

Street Outreach Program
The Gay and Lesbian Community Services Center
1213 North Highland Avenue
Los Angeles, CA 90038
(213) 464-7400

This program consists of a team of paid and volunteer staff who are out in the streets at various times throughout the week to promote the program's services. Targeted areas with concentrations of street youth have been identified. The team has been developing linkages with the Department of Children's Services, the Department of Health Services, the Hollywood Police Department, the West Hollywood Sheriff's Department, Teen Canteen and youth shelters in the area.

Temenos Youth Outreach Program
Gay and Lesbian Community Services Center
1213 North Highland Avenue
Los Angeles, CA 90038
(213) 464-7400
Youth Talkline: (213) 462-8130

The Temenos Youth Outreach Program is designed to alleviate isolation and enhance self-esteem among lesbian and gay youth. Temenos offers rap groups for young people 23 and under and operates the Gay and Lesbian Youth Talkline, which provides both emotional support and resource referrals. The program also provides workshops to any interested school, group or organization that serves young people. The Talkline is in operation Thursdays 7:00–10:00 p.m. and Fridays and Saturdays 7:00 p.m. to midnight.

Youth Eastside Services (YES)
16150 NE 8th Street
Bellevue, WA 98008
(206) 747-4937

YES provides a range of programs including education, counseling, youth employment and social development services. Since 1968, YES has been a primary provider of social services for teens and their families living in the five school districts of eastern King County. In 1985, YES became the first mainstream agency in Washington State to develop a program specifically for gay and lesbian teens. Developed and supported by an advisory committee of parents and professionals, the Gay/Lesbian Drop-In Group (GLAD) project has developed a biweekly support and education program for youth. YES can provide consultation and training services for others interested in pursuing similar efforts, working with sexual minority youth and integrating multicultural awareness into education and service delivery.

PRINT MATERIALS

Counseling Lesbian and Gay Male Youth: Their Special Lives/ Special Needs, Sage Bergstrom, MSW and Lawrence Cruz, MSW, Eds., National Network of Runaway and Youth Services, 1983.

Anthology of articles by professional youth workers, covering myths and stereotypes, the family and coming out, administration and delivery of social services and special perspectives (rural youth, cultural sensitivity and working with Third World lesbian/gay youth, implications of sex role conformity). *National Network of Runawayand Youth Services, 1400 I Street NW, Suite 330, Washington, DC 20036. Single copies $10 postpaid.*

FYI: What You Should Know About the Boston Foster Parenting Case, Office of Lesbian and Gay Concerns, Unitarian Universalist Association.

Information packet concerning a case that powerfully illustrates the impact of homophobia in some systems of foster care placement; analysis and implications. *Office of Lesbian and Gay Concerns, UUA, 25 Beacon Street, Boston, MA 02108. Single copies $1 postpaid.*

Lesbian and Gay Issues: A Resource Manual for Social Workers, Hilda Hidalgo, Travil L. Peterson and Natalie Jane Woodman, Eds., National Association of Social Workers.

From the NASW Task Force on Lesbian and Gay Issues; practical articles on knowledge and skills needed to work with gay/lesbian clients. Includes institutional intervention, meeting special needs of subgroups (i.e., youth, disabled persons, etc.) and more. *National Association of Social Workers, 7981 Eastern Avenue, Silver Spring, MD 20910. Single copies $16.95 plus $1.70 postage and handling.*

 **Legal Concerns**

See AIDS Crisis section for organizations and materials dealing with legal aspects of AIDS.

ORGANIZATIONS AND PROJECTS

American Civil Liberties Union (ACLU)
Lesbian and Gay Rights Project
132 West 43rd Street
New York, NY 10036
(212) 944-9800

The ACLU Foundation's Lesbian and Gay Rights Project fights AIDS-related discrimination and violations of privacy and civil rights, working for the eradication of sodomy laws and all forms of discrimination against lesbians and gay men.

American Civil Liberties Union of Northern California (ACLU-NC)
Gay Rights Chapter
1663 Mission Street, Suite 460
San Francisco, CA 94103
(415) 621-2493

The ACLU-NC's Gay Rights Chapter monitors AIDS discrimination issues, engages in outreach and education on issues concerning lesbians and gay men, participates in community organizing and lobbying activities and is involved in selective litigation to establish constitutional rights. Speakers are available.

Lambda Legal Defense and Education Fund (LLDEF)
666 Broadway
New York, NY 10012
(212) 995-8585

LLDEF focuses on cases concerning lesbian/gay civil rights with national precedent-setting potential in such areas as AIDS-related discrimination, employment discrimination, lesbian and gay families, sodomy law repeal and challenging race/sex discrimination within the lesbian/gay communities. LLDEF does not offer attorney referrals or routine legal work for individuals. Inquire about membership, which includes quarterly newsletter.

Midwest Committee for Military Counseling
343 South Dearborn, No. 1113
Chicago, IL 60604
(312) 939-3349

Organization experienced in providing free, confidential assistance to women and men who are serving in the military, considering military service or applying for conscientious objector status; provides specialized help for lesbians and gay men. See Print Materials, this section, for publications.

Militarism Resource Project
P.O. Box 13416
Philadelphia, PA 19101-3416
(215) 386-4875

The MRP is a national organization that does educational work on military service issues that affect low-income communities. Provides assistance to organizers and concerned community members who wish to organize around military service issues. Has considerable expertise on lesbian/gay military issues and on military policies on HIV antibody and AIDS issues.

Military Law Task Force
National Lawyers Guild
1168 Union Street, Suite 201
San Diego, CA 92101
(619) 233-1701

The MLTF is the national committee coordinating National Lawyers Guild work on draft, military and veterans issues; it is composed of attorneys, law students, legal workers and draft and military counselors throughout the U.S. A significant part of MLTF work concerns gay and lesbian rights, challenging homophobic regulations and practices within the armed services. See separate listing in AIDS Crisis section for MLTF's National Military Project on AIDS. MLTF bimonthly newsletter available. Sample copies $1.25

each; subscriptions $10/year for individuals and $20/year for institutions and organizations.

National Gay Rights Advocates (NGRA)
540 Castro Street
San Francisco, CA 94114
(415) 863-3624

NGRA focuses on lesbian/gay civil rights impact litigation, selecting cases most likely to establish positive national legal precedents in such areas as employment, immigration, couples' rights and other civil rights concerns. Fully staffed AIDS Civil Rights Project works to protect legal rights of persons who have or may have AIDS or ARC (AIDS-related complex). Computerized case files and gay law library are available for attorney advisement; NGRA is sometimes able to provide legal advice and referrals. Inquire about membership which includes quarterly newsletter.

Many communities or regions have one or more of the following organizations or agencies that may be helpful with a variety of legal issues concerning or affecting lesbian and gay youth: chapters of the American Civil Liberties Union and the National Lawyers Guild, juvenile justice projects and advocates; public interest law firms focusing on educational issues and legal referral projects.

PRINT MATERIALS

The Draft: Gay Questions, Serious Answers, Midwest Committee for Military Counseling and National Lawyers Guild Military Law Task Force and Gay Rights Task Force, 1986 (3rd edition).

Pamphlet providing clear, concise answers to questions gay and bisexual males may have about registering for the draft, registration procedures and concerns, AIDS testing, etc. (11 pp.) *Military Law Task Force, National Lawyers Guild, 1168 Union Street, No. 201, San Diego, CA 92101, or Midwest Committee for Military Counseling, 343 South Dearborn, No. 1113, Chicago, IL 60604. Single copies 40 cents plus 15% postage and handling; inquire for bulk rates.*

Fighting Back: Lesbian and Gay Draft, Military and Veterans Issues, Midwest Committee for Military Counseling and Military Law Task Force, National Committee to Combat Women's Oppression and Gay Rights Task Force of the National Lawyers Guild.

Comprehensive manual for lawyers and counselors; includes analysis of pertinent regulations for the military, Selective Service and Veterans Administration and step-by-step guidance for draft, military and vets' cases; offers answers to basic questions about military policy on homosexuality and detailed explanations for those using or challenging the regulations. *Military Law Task Force, National Lawyers Guild, 1168 Union Street, No. 201, San Diego, CA 92101, or Midwest Committee for Military Counseling, 343 South Dearborn, No. 1113, Chicago, IL 60604. Single copies $14.25 plus $2 shipping; add $1 for first class postage. Inquire for bulk rates.*

Surviving Witchhunts, developed by the Midwest Committee for Military Counseling and the Military Law Task Force of the National Lawyers Guild, 1985.

Leaflet for lesbians and gay men in the armed forces succinctly summarizing their rights and providing basic advice on how to avoid incriminating themselves if investigated by military authorities. *Midwest Committee for Military Counseling, 343 South Dearborn, No. 1113, Chicago IL 60605, or Military Law Task Force, National Lawyers Guild, 1168 Union Street, No. 201, San Diego, CA 92102. Single copies 25 cents each; inquire for bulk rates.*

DATE DUE

~~JUL 26 16~~			
AUG 1 1 2013			

Demco, Inc. 38-293